MW00803384

PJ HARVEY was born in Dorset in 1969. Her debut
poetry collection, *The Hollow of the Hand*, was created
in collaboration with photographer Seamus Murphy.

Harvey was awarded an MBE for services to music as well
as an Honorary Degree in Music from Goldsmiths University.
She has received numerous Grammy Award nominations, has
scored music for several TV, film and theatrical productions,
and is the only artist to have won the Mercury Prize twice,
with her albums *Stories from the City, Stories from the Sea*
and *Let England Shake*.

Also by PJ Harvey

The Hollow of the Hand

PJ HARVEY

PICADOR

First published 2022 by Picador
an imprint of Pan Macmillan
6 Briset Street, London EC1M 5NR
EU representative: Macmillan Publishers Ireland Ltd,
Macmillan Publishers Ireland Limited, 1st Floor, The Liffey Trust Centre,
117–126 Sheriff Street Upper, Dublin 1 D01 YC43
Associated companies throughout the world
www.panmacmillan.com

ISBN 978-1-5290-6311-0

Copyright © PJ Harvey 2022

The right of PJ Harvey to be identified as the
author of this work has been asserted by her in accordance
with the Copyright, Designs and Patents Act 1988.

All rights reserved. No part of this publication may be reproduced,
stored in a retrieval system, or transmitted, in any form, or by any means
(electronic, mechanical, photocopying, recording or otherwise)
without the prior written permission of the publisher.

Pan Macmillan does not have any control over, or any responsibility for,
any author or third-party websites referred to in or on this book.

5 7 9 8 6

A CIP catalogue record for this book is available from the British Library.

Printed and bound by TJ Books Ltd, Padstow, Cornwall PL28 8RW

This book is sold subject to the condition that it shall not, by way of
trade or otherwise, be lent, hired out, or otherwise circulated without
the publisher's prior consent in any form of binding or cover other than
that in which it is published and without a similar condition including
this condition being imposed on the subsequent purchaser.

Visit **www.picador.com** to read more about all our books
and to buy them. You will also find features, author interviews and
news of any author events, and you can sign up for e-newsletters
so that you're always first to hear about our new releases.

Contents

Note on the Text

While it draws on elements of my own West Country childhood, especially its landscape and folklore, this book is a work of the imagination.

The poem is written in the Dorset dialect, and its English translation appears to its left. The more dense the dialect, the darker the typeface of the translation.

While a full glossary is supplied at the end of the book, notes on local flora, fauna, folklore, etymology and literary sources appear below the poems.

— PJH

Orlam

Prayer at the Gate
January 1st, Gore Woods

As childhood died the new-born year
made The Soldier reappear.

The ash embowered night and day
as at the five-bar gate she prayed;

Wyman-Elvis, am I worthy?
Wyman, speak your world to me.

Elms unveiled in secret places
a thousand ghostie-children's faces

and rain-mist shrouded in its cloak
lost lane, river, brook and oak,

and all souls under Orlam's reign
made passage for the *born again*.

So look behind and look before
at life a-knocking at death's door

and reach towards your dark-haired Lord
forever bleeding with The Word.

Prayer at the Gate

January 1st, Gore Woods

As childhood died the new-born year
made The Soldier reappear.

The ash embowered night and day
as at the five-bar gate she prayed;

Wyman-Elvis, am I worthy?
Wyman, speak your wordle to me.

Elms unveiled in secret places
a thousand soonere-children's faces

and drisk enshrouded in its cloak
holway, river, brook and oak,

and all souls under Orlam's reign
made passage for the *born again*.

So look behind and look before
at life a-knocking at death's door

and teake towards your dark-haired Lord
forever bleeding with The Word.

January

In which we meet Orlam, the all-seeing eye of the dead lamb Mallory-Sonny, who introduces us to the dwellers of the West Country village of UNDERWHELEM, home to nine-year-old Ira-Abel Rawles who lives with her parents, Chalmers-Adam and Lola-Effie, and her brother Kane-Jude on a sheep farm.

Orlam Tells the Whole Story

Ira-Abel Rawles, 9
Second-born child of heart murmurs.
Lives with a forest of intimates.
Sleeps with eyes half open.
Stows an ash leaf in her shoe.
White bride of Wyman.

Wyman-Elvis, 21
Ghost-warrior from The Ransham Rebellion?
The King's apparition?
He bleeds from the throat on a bed of mullein.
Utters The Word to our girl in white —
Love Me Tender, *till the end of time.*

Red Post Ghosts — The Ransham Dead
Pitch-boiled, gelded, hung, cut up;
Fated whistlers of the wood.
Their tune? Washed in the Blood.
Wyman's shadow-soldier brothers;
Penne, Young, Wheelhouse Brown. Nine others.

Kane-Jude Rawles, 12
Firstborn son. Fed rabbit-brains to stop his crying.
Hardworking hero praised by elders.
Marries for land. Turns crop farmer.
Eats blackberries in October.
Dies of fever on a bed of pigeon feathers.

Orlam Tells the Whole Story

Ira-Abel Rawles, 9

Second-born child of heart murmurs.
Bides with a forest of intimates.
Sleeps with eyes half open.
Stows an ash leaf in her shoe.
White bride of Wyman.

Wyman-Elvis, 21

Ghost-warrior from The Ransham Rebellion?
The King's apparition?
He bleeds from the throat on a bed of mullein.
Utters The Word to our girl in white —
Love Me Tender, *till the end of time.*

Red Post Sooneres — The Ransham Dead

Pitch-boiled, gelded, hung, cut up;
Fated whistlers of the wood.
Their tuen? Washed in the Blood.
Wyman's shadow-soldier brothers;
Penne, Young, Wheelhouse Brown. Nine others.

Kane-Jude Rawles, 12

Firstborn son. Fed bunker's brains to stop his crying.
Hard-worken hero praised by elders.
Marries for land. Turns crop farmer.
Eats blackberries in October.
Dies of fever on a bed of woodculver.

Chalmers-Adam Rawles, 44

Liver-shot father. Silent sot.
Bad shepherd. Master's swagger
Till a crooked nail makes him lame.
Half-drowns in the sheep dip.
Raven pecks his window.

Mallory-Sonny, 40 days

Behold The Lamb, I am, I am!
Black-faced, outcast, sickly twin,
Fostered by our heroine.
Poor little lambie cries, Mammy! A storytelling of rooks
Pecks out his eye. THIS eye.

Orlam

Remade from Mallory
I ever-see my kingdom
One eye high in The Ultimate Elm;
Protector of Ira-Abel,
And oracle of UNDERWHELEM.

John Forsey — Devil's-Cock, 64

Gate-keeper, forester, lank hair red
As rotting leaves. Rammish ash-killer,
Bogey-man. Fiend? Horny beast?
Blocks road with stones at Blaggot's Knowle.
Dies in the deed. Rises again. Sperm is cold.

Chalmers-Adam Rawles, 44

A-cothed father. Silent sot.
Bad shepherd. Master's zwail
Till crooked nail makes laminger.
Near-drowsy in the sheep dip.
Raven pecks his window.

Mallory-Sonny, 40 days

Behold The Lamb, I am, I am!
Black-faced, outcast, sickly twin,
Fostered by our heroine.
Poor little lambie cries, Mammy! *A storytelling of rooks*
Pecks out his eye. THIS *eye.*

Orlam

Remade from Mallory
I ever-see my kingdom
One eye high in The Ultimate Elm;
Protector of Ira-Abel,
And oracle of UNDERWHELEM.

John Forsey — Ooser-Rod, 64

Gate-keeper, forester, lank hair red
As rotting leaves. Rammish ash-killer,
Bogey-man. Wurse? Horny beast?
Blocks road with stones at Blaggot's Knowle.
Dies in the deed. Rises again. Sperm is cold.

Ash-Wraiths

Boys and girls come with a call
Under the silver southern ball.
Shining eyes, tiny cries;
Hark the green leaves' hidden laughter.
All who hear are charmed thereafter.

Aaron-Unwin White, 12

Not-friend neighbour of Clap Corner.
Albino, lash-less, pink-eyed tough.
Beasty-boy with fleecy-fingers,
Caught with cock in a ewe's muff.
Breeds a doo-lally daughter.

Lola-Effie Rawles née Colby, 39

Woman from the dark farmstead.
Wife of miscarriage, mother of un-love,
Falls milkless. Wanders the high downs
Looking for hoar-stones.
Held in The House of Traps.

Elda-Mary Rawles

Chalmers's Mammy, Beloved Lady,
Sea of bitterness. Grandma.
Old and wise protector.
Forever this ghostie's tune: Hush-A-Bye, Don't you Cry,
Hovers in the hollow lane under the moon.

Ash-Wraiths

Boys and girls come with a call
Under the silver southern ball.
Shining eyes, tiny cries;
Hark the green leaves' hidden laughter.
All who hear are charmed thereafter.

Aaron-Unwin White, 12

Not-friend neighbour of Clap Corner.
Albino, lash-less, pink-eyed huff.
Beasty-boy with fleecy-fingers,
Caught with rod in a ewe's muff.
Breeds a de-da daughter.

Lola-Effie Rawles née Colby, 39

Woman from the dark farmstead.
Wife of miscarriage, mother of un-love,
Falls a-zew. Wanders the high downs
Looking for hoar-stones.
Held in The House of Traps.

Elda-Mary Rawles

Chalmers's Mammy, Beloved Lady,
Sea of bitterness. Gramm'er.
Old and wise protector.
Forever this soonere's tuen: Hush-A-Bye, Don't you Cry,
Hovers in the holway under the moon.

The Bowditches of Dogwell
Emery, 61; sugar disease leaves half a man.
Myra, 57, drunk by noon, taps
The hatch of The Golden Fleece.
Emerson-Dogger, 37,
Bumps four daughters in The Red Shed.

Mrs. Forsey – Sloven-Mole
Rancid, daft and going blind.
Birch-whipped by The Devil's-Cock.
Coos to her log baby.
Stands naked at the net curtains;
Don't be, don't be, didn't, didn't.

The Bowditches of Dogwell

Emery, 61; sugar disease leaves half a man.
Myra, 57, soused by noon, taps
The hatch of The Golden Fleece.
Emerson-Dogger, 37,
Bumps four daughters in The Red Shed.

Mrs. Forsey – Slommock-Want

Rafty, ne-na, going dark.
Birch-whipped by The Ooser-Rod.
Croodles to her log baby.
Stands naked at the net curtains;
B'aint, b'aint, didden, didden.

Stows an ash leaf – it was believed that if a maiden placed ash leaves under her pillow, she would have prophetic dreams of her future lover, or that to carry one with you brings you good fortune; *mullein* – a tall, stiff flowered, woolly plant, also known as 'soldier's tears'; *bunker's brains* – if you feed rabbit or hare brains to a troublesome infant it will cure them; *blackberries in October* – you should not eat blackberries after September as the devil spits on them; *bed of woodculver* – you cannot die peacefully on a wood pigeon's feathers (they should never be used to stuff a bed or cushions); *Raven pecks . . .* – any bird that taps at the window or flies into the pane of an invalid's room is a harbinger of death; *Poor little lambie* – from 'All The Pretty Little Horses', US folksong, lullaby; *Ooser-Rod* – a devil's penis, abnormally large; *The Dorset Ooser* (/ˈoʊsər/) – also oose or wu'se. A mask with grim jaws, put on with a cow's skin to frighten folk, an arch-fiend, a devil; *Hush-A-Bye, Don't you Cry* – taken from a song ('Alabama C— Song') often sung innocently as a lullaby to Dorset children in the 1970s by the older generation

Birth of Ira-Abel

I knelt to eat
the inflamed brain

of the false morel
and the woods took me in.

The grouse beat their wings
on a rotten log;

the wood pigeons, *Hit
the rooooooad Jack*;

the crows wove a cloak
of plaited sedge

in which I fled across
Great Ink Field

scratching at my skin,
uprooting black stalks

to write this.

Birth of Ira-Abel

I knelt to eat
the inflamed brain

of the false morel
and the woods took me in.

The grouse beat their wings
on a rotten log;

the woodculvers, *Hit
the rooooooad Jack*;

the crows wove a cloak
of plaited sedge

in which I fled across
Great Ink Field

scratching at my skin,
uprooting black stalks

to write this.

Hit the Road Jack – a Percy Mayfield song; *Great
Ink Field* –a large cornfield in UNDERWHELEM

Naming: Ira

The chosen singular.
The ninth letter as in 'mind', as in 'bird'.

A raw start of air,
a crooked choler.

Staring creature of the forest inner
I am. A compulsion.

Lightfoot girl with horrid curl.
Restless haruspex.

Two hacks
at the earth with an axe.

Naming: Ira

The chosen singular.
The ninth letter as in 'mind', as in 'bird'.

A raw start of air,
a crooked choler.

Glowing creature of the forest inner
I am. A compulsion.

Litty girl with horrid curl.
Restless haruspex.

Two hacks
at the eth with an axe.

Ira – watchful, vigilant; *horrid curl* – 'There was
a Little Girl' by Henry Wadsworth Longfellow

Naming: Abel

The primary letter as in 'path', as in 'bad'.
The fundamental murder.

An unbaptised breath,
a bound, a stumble,

an expelled alpha.
First seed.

An earth-hole of stood-up bones.
Lonesome chaser of the absolute acre.

The five-wounds. A ladder.
A vapour.

Naming: Abel

The primary letter as in 'path', as in 'bad'.
The fundamental murder.

An unbaptised breath,
a bundle, a stumble,

an expelled alpha.
First seed.

An eth hole of bones a-stooded.
Lwonesome chaser of the absolute acre.

The five-wounds. A ladder.
A vapour.

Abel – breath, transitoriness, a vapour, a great meadow,
a grassy place; *The five-wounds* – in Christian theology
the letter 'A' refers to the five wounds of Christ; *ladder*
– the letter 'A' as a means of spiritual ascension

Happy Families

Father Rawles, the rancid reaper,
Had a wife but couldn't keep her,
Had a daughter-not-bo-peeper:
Weepy-dreeper, walking-sleeper.
Lost her lamb and lost her brother,
In a cow's afterbirth found her mother.

Happy Families

Father Rawles, the rafty reaper
Had a wife but couldn' keep 'er,
Had a daughter-not-bo-peeper:
Weepy-dreeper, walking-sleeper.
Lost her lamb an' lost her brother,
In a fowel found her mother.

Happy Families — a traditional British card game
featuring illustrations of fictional families of four

UNDERWHELEM

Foul village in a hag-ridden hollow.
All ways to it winding, all roads to it narrow.

Bedevilled bog, veiled in fog,
perverse, furtive, rank with seepings:

Jeyes Fluid, slurry, sweat and pus,
anus grease, squitters, jizz and blood.

Breeder of asthma, common warts, ringworm.
Ward of ancient occupations;

ploughshares rusting in the brambles,
half-walls, smuggler's runs and ditches,

blackened hearthstones, ulcerous lullabies;
Mummy's going to smack you if you don't . . .

The crossroads a red hanging-post
to GOAT HILL — RANSHAM — OVERWHELEM.

Three hoar-stones, one Golden Fleece
connected by a single Riddle.

Grandpa blackthorn bent by wind.
Shabby ewes trying to die.

A haunted wood in the realm of an Eye.
A farm of hooks with a rout of Rawles:

UNDERWHELEM

Voul village in a hag-ridden hollow.
All ways to it winding, all roads to it narrow.

Auverlooked bog, veiled in vog,
thirtover, undercreepen, rank with seepings:

Jeyes Fluid, slurry, zweat and pus,
anus greaze, squitters, jizz and blood.

Breeder of asthma, common warts, ringworm.
Ward of ancient occupations;

ploughshares rusting in the brembles,
half-walls, smuggler's runs and ditches,

blackened heth stones, lured lullabies;
Mummy's going to smack you if you don't . . .

The crossroads a red hanging-post
to GOAT HILL — RANSHAM — OVERWHELEM.

Three hoar-stones, one Golden Fleece
connected by a single Riddle.

Gramf'er blackthorn bent by wind.
Shabby mothers trying to die.

A haunted wood in the realm of an Eye.
A farm of hooks with a rout of Rawles:

a mother of sorrow, a fatherlike fiend,
an oddball son and his inward friend,

and a not-girl born amongst them:
fouling her fig in the forest,

honking a conk-load of creosote,
downing a dram of diazinon,

flaying a fleece-full of maggots,
gorging a gutful of entrails,

crunching the scabs of her grievance,
hoarding the horrible omens,

bearing the burden of world.

a mother of sorrow, a farterous fiend,
a rumstick son and his inward friend,

and a not-gurrel born amongst them:
fouling her fig in the forest,

honking a conk-load of creosote,
downing a dram of diazinon,

flaying a fleeceful of maggots,
gorging a gutful of entrails,

scrounching her scabs o' engripement,
hoarding the horrible heissens,

bearing the burden of wordle.

Mummy's going to smack you if you don't – from 'Alabama C—
Song'; *The Golden Fleece* – UNDERWHELEM'S pub; *Riddle*
– UNDERWHELEM'S river; *Rawles* – family name, from
the Old Norse "Ráðúlfr": Norse elements "rað", counsel,
advice, and "wolf"; *diazinon* – active ingredient in sheep dip

Twigs

One

Look at Ira:
Staring so!
The more you write
The less you'll know

Twiddicks

Woone

Onlook Ira:
Glow, glow, glow!
The more you scratch
The less you'll know

FEBRUARY

Ira's bottle-fed lamb, Mallory-Sonny, is killed by the rooks. We enter Ira's sanctuary, the haunted Gore Woods. It's time to ring the lambs' tails and testicles on Hook Farm. Brother Kane cuts off Ira's hair and Ira has a premonition of her death in childhood. Kane creates his invisible inward friend, James Michael Adrian; rejected by Kane, Ira finds a dying soldier — Wyman-Elvis — in the woods on Valentine's Day. He is one of The Ransham Rebellion from the English civil war who now haunt Gore Woods. His throat is cut and bleeding. He becomes Ira's first love, Christ and King, and bearer of The Word.

Twigs
Two

Hunger Moon at morning hangs,
Cracks his gob to flash a fang.
Death descends to butt with Birth.
Shiver ye who live on earth!

Twiddicks

Two

Hunger Moon at morning hangs,
Cracks 'es gap to flash a fang.
Death descends to butt wi' Birth.
Biver ye that bide on eth!

Hunger Moon – the second full moon of the year

The World Is

Gore Woods

I

Frigid winter, fertile spring
lusty woods awakening
February fever fondles Gore,
rubs him with a saucy spore.
Fur and feather dwellers wed
gather bark for nooky beds
they all sing along the breeze,
Umpteen little cunties please!

Horny pigeons strut and coo
slugs and snails a-smear their goo
every copse a copping-host –
Blaggot's Knowle to Hanging Post
all woodpeckers throb and thrum
peewit pimps and bumbles hum,
Glory hole or up the bum?
Everybody wants to come!

The Wordle Is

Gore Woods

I

Frigid winter, fertile spring
lusty woods awakening
Feverell fever fondles Gore,
rubs en with a saucy spore
Fur and feather dwellers wed
gather scroff for nooky beds
all 'em zing a-long a breeze,
Umpteen little cunties pleeeazze!

Horny culvers strut and coo
slugs and snails a-smame their goo
every copse a copping-host –
Blaggot's Knowle to Hanging Post
peckers throb and spotters thrum
peewit pimps and dumbles hum,
Glory hole or up zee bum?
Everybody wantz to come!

II

Magpie fiend and cuckoo spit
robin with his breast of fate
ash twigs stuffed into my sock
to keep away that robin-cock

Meagre month, your sorrow sowed
laid my eyes upon the toad
spit on him and sling a stone
lest he brings his evil home

Bloodless bells of Candlemas:
snowdrops in their spastic hats
someone picks them, takes them in
sets a curse on all within

Pipistrelle by the light of day,
ill-luck preacher: crimson rays
maul the morning; malice spills
over new-borns on the hills

Sickly spores are on the breeze
lambs' tails wither in the leas
under earth the mole-hill slaves
must be readying the graves

Sun's a cunty, crimson whore,
a bloated tear of hogget gore
blinding Ira, where I stand
grieving gut-strings for The Lamb

II

Devil's bird and goocoo spume
reddick with 'es breast o' doom
aish-a-twiddick in my sock
to keep away thik reddick-cock

Meagre month, yer sorrow sowed
laid my eyes upon the twoad
spet on en and sling a stone
lest 'e brings 'es evil hwome

Bloodless bells of Candlemas:
milk flowers in their spastic hats
somen picks em, takes em in
sets a curse on all within

Vlittermouse by light of day,
ill-luck preacher: crimson rays
maul the morning; malice spills
over new-borns on the hills

Sickly spores are on the breeze
lambs' tails wither on the leaze
under eth the want-heave slaves
must be readying the graves

Zun's a red-bread, crimson whore,
a bloated tear of hogget gore
blinding Ira, where I stand
grieving gut-strings for The Lamb

Sex and death all roundabout
Sonny with his eyes pecked out
Scoff the blow-flies and the worms,
This is how the world turns

Sex and death all roundabout
Sonny with 'es eyes pecked out
Scoff the vlesh vlee and the yis,
This is how the wordle is

reddick – the robin can be seen as a bird of 'ill omen', a harbinger
of death; *aish-a-twiddick* – ash twig (in British folklore the ash was
credited with a range of protective and healing properties, most
frequently related to child health); *twoad* – toad (whenever you
found a toad, you had to spit on it or throw a stone at it to keep off
its evil effects); *milk flower* – snowdrop; snowdrops were considered
unlucky if brought indoors; *zun's a red-bread, crimson . . .* – 'red sky at
night, shepherd's delight: red sky at morning, shepherd's warning'

Way down yonda', down in the medder
There's a poor little lambie.
Bees an' the butterflies peckin' out his eyes . . .

Mercy on Mallory

Unlucky lad —
your tender gaze
eased my days.

Poor runt,
black sacrifice,
you I raised,

called your name
till the rooks ripped down
February's dawn —

I found your brains
by some roofing iron
and a pen of thorns

where blowflies
supped your blood.
The ewes stared.

Your death
opens the gates
to the dark world.

Way down yonda', down in the medder
There's a poor little lambie.
Bees an' the butterflies peckin' out his eyes . . .

Mercy on Mallory

Unlucky lad –
your tender gaze
eased my days.

Nesseltripe,
blatch sacrifice,
you I raised,

called your name
till the rooks ripped down
February's dawn –

I found your brains
by some roofing iron
and a pleck of thorns

where vlesh vlees
supped your blood.
Shabby mothers stared.

Your death
opens the gates
to the dark wordle.

Way down yonda' . . . – from 'All the Pretty Little Horses', US folksong, lullaby

Gore Woods

Dirt on your face
and twigs for tears
your future was here
in the endless ash trees
searching for corpses
to bring to the pen

swollen badgers
the silk purses
of squirrels and mice,
their mouths inlaid
with bluebottle eggs
naked, new-hatched rooks
and an empire of maggots
in a fawn's head

In the violet half-light
you learnt the truth
of the blade and the axe
as you stood in the soft mulch
by a car battery
a jerry-can
the electric fence

Gore Woods

Dirt on your face
and twiddicks for tears
your future was here
in the endless ash trees
searching for corpses
to bring to the pen

swollen badgers
the silk purses
of squirrels and mice,
their mouths inlaid
with vlesh vlee eggs
naked, new-hatched rooks
and an empire of maggots
in a fawn's head

In the violet half-light
you learnt the truth
of the blade and the axe
as you stood in the soft mulch
by a car battery
a jerry-can
the electric fence

Stations of Ira-Abel
Gore Woods

One: Ash Trees

    Shameless hermaphrodites.
    Hosts of a thousand shining eyes,
    Bestowers of winged keys,
    Crowned followers of light.

Two: Swamp Laurel

    Chapel of the acid bog.
    Thousand-headed violet web.
    Waxy-fingered net to hang
    Bad wishes in a basket:
    Deciduous tooth, hair lock,
    Blood gauze.

Three: Brook

    Clay-soft consoler,
    Chanteuse, nurse.
    Psalm of the palms
    Cupping and sipping.

Four: Orlam

    Magnified eyeball
    Of the lustrate Lamb,
    Now gloriole-crowned
    in The Ultimate Elm.

Stations of Ira-Abel

Gore Woods

Woone: Ash Trees
> Shameless hermaphrodites.
> Hosts of a thousand shining eyes,
> Bestowers of winged keys,
> Crowned followers of light.

Two: Swamp Laurel
> Chapel of the acid bog.
> Thousand-headed violet web.
> Waxy-fingered net to hang
> Bad wishes in a basket:
> Deciduous tooth, hair lock,
> Blood gauze.

Dree: Brook
> Clay-soft consoler,
> Chanteuse, nurse.
> Psalm of the palms
> Cupping and sipping.

Vower: Orlam
> Magnified eyeball
> Of the lustrate Lamb,
> Now gloriole-crowned
> in The Ultimate Elm.

Five: Rhododendron
>Advancing nebula
>Of poison.
>Impenetrable
>Rubber foreigner.

Six: Dead Oak
>Tower of hedera,
>House of wormwood.
>Scored with epitaphs,
>Full of small voices.

Seven: Labyrinth
>Intimate web
>In the realm
>Of The Lamb.
>At its eye
>A child's shrine –
>A fawn-skull
>Still furred,
>A palace of worms,
>An axe with two heads.

Eight: Hollow Lane
>Screened with ferns,
>Underpass for offerings
>And words between worlds.
>Smuggler's run –
>Shelter from the Forsey-man.

Vive: Rhododendron
>Advancing nebula
>Of poison.
>Impenetrable
>Rubber foreigner.

Zix: Dead Oak
>Tower of hedera,
>House of wormwood.
>Scored with epitaphs,
>Full of small voices.

Zebm: Labyrinth
>Intimate web
>In the realm
>Of The Lamb.
>At its eye
>A child's shrine –
>A fawn-skull
>Still furred,
>A palace of worms,
>An axe with two heads.

Aïght: Holway
>Screened with ferns,
>Underpass for offerings
>And words between worlds.
>Smuggler's run –
>Shelter from the Forsey-man.

Nine: Rookery

Black clamour
Ascends through the ash
Roaring the forecast:
Dead kids coming!
Dead kids coming!

Ten: Grouse Pen

Friend-catcher
For little note-leavers –
Chain-letter brethren,
Ghostly children,
The cold-at-supper-time,
Who can't go home.

Eleven: Fairy Ring

White-lily limbs
Nipped by the blackthorns.
Dainty imps
Weave lullabies
For the Ash-Wraiths, for Ira
And the dying Soldier.

Twelve: Cast Calf

Premature, piebald,
Misty-eyed mourner,
Evermore o'erlooking
Cowleaze and Gore.
Fixed to the fork

46

Nine: Rookery
Black clamour
Ascends through the ash
Roaring the forecast:
Dead kids coming!
Dead kids coming!

Ten: Grouse Pen
Friend-catcher
For little note-leavers —
Chain-letter brethren,
Chalky children,
The cold-at-supper-time,
Who can't go home.

Elebm:Veäry Ring
White-lily limbs
Nipped by the blackthorns.
Dainty imps
Weave lullabies
For the Ash-Wraiths, for Ira
And the dying Soldier.

Twelve: Cast Calf
Premature, piebald,
Misty-eyed mourner,
Evermore o'erlooking
Cowleaze and Gore.
Fixed to the fork

Of the maiden ash,
Head pointing east,
Weeping his warning,
With a blue, swollen tongue;
Birth your calves early
And they will be hung!
Birth your calves early
And they will be hung!

Of the maiden ash,
Head pointing east,
Weeping his warning,
With a blue, swollen tongue;
Cast your calves early
And they will be hung!
Cast your calves early
And they will be hung!

veäry ring – rings of fungi that come from the dancing of fairies;
cast – prematurely born; farmers used to place a prematurely
born calf in the fork of a maiden ash, head pointing east to
prevent other cows in the herd from casting their calves

Little Bi-sheep
sung to the tune of 'Little Bo-Peep'

It hardly hurts at all, he said,
But Chalmers could well be lying;
Turning the boy-lambs upside down,
Jabbing with anti-toxin.

I heave a sigh, and wipe my eye,
And squeeze the elastrator;
I feed their little balls through
Rubber bands with shaking fingers.

He lifts the lambs, then cracks his crook
To drive them to the sheep-run;
Where they lay on their backs, and they bleat and they kick
And they roll their eyes to heaven.

What are they now? Not-girl, not-boy?
I feel myself just like them.
I wait three weeks for the Lenten moon
Then over the hills go rambling,

And take the shrivelled tails and balls
In a Gateway bag to the forest.
I sing them a song, but can't pin them back on
But Chalmers' death I promise.

Little Bi-sheep

sung to the tune of 'Little Bo-Peep'

It hardly hurts at all, he said,
But Chalmers could well be lying;
Turning the boy-lambs upside down,
Jabbing with anti-toxin.

I heave a sigh, and wipe my eye,
And squeeze the elastrator;
I feed their little balls through
Rubber bands with shaking fingers.

He lifts the lambs, then cracks his crook
To drive them to the grotten;
Where they lay on their backs, and they blether and kick
And they roll their eyes to heaven.

What are they now? Not-girl, not-boy?
I feel myself just like them.
I wait three weeks for the Lenten moon
Then over the hills go rambling,

And take the shrivelled tails and balls
In a Gateway bag to the forest.
I sing them a song, but can't pin them back on
But Chalmers' death I promise.

elastrator – pliers used to place a tight latex ring around the
base of the scrotum; *Lenten moon* – the full moon in March

Black Saturday
February 11th

Kane-Jude shaved me a no. 1.
I hung the hair in the hawthorn.

We collected bogies in a jam-jar
to melt and mould into a brain,

then rubbed our groins on the carpet
till we got that *gone* feeling watching Jim'll Fix It.

Kanius Maximus gave me his Y-fronts.
Made toilet-roll tube telescopes

and went on a reconnaissance
for German soldiers in Blaggot's Copse.

Then Kane-Jude killed me with this name,
James-Michael-Adrian,

his invisible friend,
who's a brigadier, a rock singer

and a Liverpool FC football player.
Kane left to play with J.M.A.

Threw Waxen from the window upside down,
threw Crundels in the waterfall.

Black Saturday

February 11th

Kane-Jude shaved me a no. 1.
I hung the hair in the hawthorn.

We collected bogies in a jam-jar
to melt and mould into a brain,

then rubbed our groins on the carpet
till we got that *gone* feeling watching Jim'll Fix It.

Kanius Maximus gave me his Y-fronts.
Made toilet-roll tube telescopes

and went on a reconnaissance
for German soldiers in Blaggot's Copse.

Then Kane-Jude killed me with this name,
James-Michael-Adrian,

his invisible friend,
who's a brigadier, a rock singer

and a Liverpool FC football player.
Kane left to play with J.M.A.

Threw Waxen from the window upside down,
threw Crundels in the waterfall.

Whirled till I fainted on the roof of the army den.
Watched the moon block out the sun

like God's good eye
forever closing.

Whirled till I fainted on the roof of the army den.
Watched the moon block out the sun

like God's good eye
forever closing.

Waxen & Crundels — the cats (*waxen crundels* — enlarged
tonsils, glands of the neck)

Cutting with Kane

Maximus Kane
cut off my curls
with unsharpened shears.

Down Gorey lane
I carried my curls
in Cluedo-lid, tears.

I hung them in hawthorn,
I sang them a nine-song,
one for each year.

Till magpie-bird, hateborn,
snatched them, and Dorset
a-rang with his jeer;

Death to the sheep-girl!
Death to the sheep-girl
Before end of year!

And so as it's forewarned
by magpie's foredooming:
the end of me nears.

Cutting with Kane

Maximus Kane
cut off my curdles
with unsharpened shears.

Down Gorey lane
I carried my curdles
in Cluedo-lid, tears.

I hung em in hawthorn,
I sang em a nine-song,
one for each year.

Till chattermag, hateborn,
snatched em an' Darzet
a'rang with his jeer;

Death to the sheep-gurrel!
Death to the sheep-gurrel
Avore end o' year!

And so as 'tis vorewarn
by chattermag's heissen,
the end of I nears.

Hair was never to be carelessly thrown away, because if it was
used for lining a magpie's nest you would be dead within a year

Things I Found in Gore Woods: February 12th

A mole's fur-sack,
all shovel and snout,
pin-prick eyes
and blood at his mouth.
Pressed it to my common wart.

Things I Found in Gore Woods: February 12th

A want's fur-sack,
all shovel and snout,
pin-prick eyes
and blood at his mouth.
Pressed it to my common wart.

want – mole; if you rub a wart with the blood of a small
animal such as a mole, mouse or a cat, the wart will disappear

Things I Found in Gore Woods: February 13th

A dog fox
snared at the neck
by a poor wire
in the north east corner
that took two days to die.

Things I Found in Gore Woods: February 13th

A dog fox
snared at the neck
by a poor wire
in the north east corner
that took two days to die.

Things I Found in Gore Woods: February 14th

A young soldier
with a gash in his neck
who tried to beg
and through the blood
it sounded like *Love Me Tender.*

Things I Found in Gore Woods: February 14th

A young soldier
with a gash in his neck
who tried to beg
and through the blood
it sounded like *Love Me Tender.*

MARCH

At the gateway to the year, the lamb Mallory-Sonny tells his story. Ira turns to look back at her childhood and gives thanks to the woods and to Wyman-Elvis. We meet John Forsey — gatekeeper, forester and flasher. Ira makes a poison charm for James Michael Adrian. It's time to dip the sheep, and Ira puts a curse on her father. We meet her neighbours, the Bowditches of Dogwell. Orlam, the all-seeing eye, tells us how he made it to his lookout post, The Ultimate Elm, and of his absolute dedication to Ira-Abel.

Twigs
Three

Hide-and-seek with bumblebee,
Fallow-hoof and badger-claw.
When the starling and the finch appear
The gateway opens to the year.

Twiddicks

Dree

Hidy-buck wi' dumbledore,
Fallow-hoof and badger-claw.
When the stare and twink appear,
Gi'es the gateway to the year.

Sonny to the Blind World

Mallory-Sonny Tells His Story

I am the one born to die.
Once, the poor little lambie crying, Mammy!
Once the second-born frail twin
Black under January's failing moon.

My mother, her burden gone,
Did not lick my yellow wounds,
And winter's cragged light
Cut me down in the bog.

I lived until my twentieth moon
When the mouthy rooks jabbed down
To empty my head in readiness,
Spread my gut-strings,

Splay the radius of my days
And erase all I'd seen.
The ewes gazed
But did not intervene.

I rolled my eye home
To a swathe-song of love:
Come on you stranger,
You legend, you martyr,

Sonny to the Dark Wordle

Mallory-Sonny Tells His Story

I am the one born to die.
Once, the poor little lambie crying, Mammy!
Once the second-born frail twin
Black under January's failing moon.

My mother, her burden gone,
Did not lick my yellow wounds,
And winter's cragged light
Cut me down in the puxy.

I lived until my twentieth moon
When the black bards jabbed down
To empty my head in readiness,
Spread my gut-strings,

Splay the radius of my days
And erase all I'd seen.
Shabby mothers gazed
But did not intervene.

I rolled my eye home
To a swathe-song of love:
Come on you stranger,
You legend, you martyr,

And rose from the sedge grass to The Ultimate Elm,
As tallest talisman, magnetic moon, pansophic sphere.
Re-met the dark world of beast and man,
With the coffin of my eye.

And rose from the zedgemocks to The Ultimate Elm,
As tallest talisman, magnetic moon, pansophic sphere.
Re-met the dark world of beast and man,
With the coffin of my eye.

second-born frail twin / Black — it was unlucky if the first-
born lamb was black, unluckier still if the first-born were
black twins; *come on you stranger, you legend, you martyr*
— from 'Shine On You Crazy Diamond' by Pink Floyd

Oh that I were
Where I would be,
Then would I be
Where I am not;
But where I am
There I must be,
And where I would be
I can not.

Childhood

Hook Farm bent my infancy.
I fled through the back door
for the company of Gore Woods,
its ghosts, cow parsley and soft moss.
There I wept intimacies
into crypts of bracken and fern.

Toadstools, Jew's ears
and cuckoo spit sustained
me through UNDERWHELEM –
a west country misty outstep
with three hoar-stones,
The Golden Fleece and The Red Post.

Oh that I were
Where I would be,
Then would I be
Where I am not;
But where I am
There I must be,
And where I would be
I can not.

Childhood

Hook Farm bent my infancy.
I fled through the back door
for the company of Gore Woods,
its sooneres, eltroot and soft meesh.
There I wept intimacies
into crypts of bracken and fern.

Twoad's meat, Jew's ears
and goocoo spettle sustained
me through UNDERWHELEM –
a west country misty outstep
with three hoar-stones,
The Golden Fleece and The Red Post.

Tender necromancer, I lay
with corpses in my lime-pit
begging them answer,
then scratched their spells
in the oak's-skin under
the stare of Orlam.

Ira, you seer, you
sleepwalker, I see you
stumbling in outsized boots
through the wrong era
cradling the pale blue
sick-bowl of childhood.

Yet you shall meet *Him*,
the eternally bleeding Soldier.
You – a shepherdess who cannot
whistle, who only ever saw
one for sorrow, a not-girl,
not-boy. Bride of his Word.

Nesh necromancer, I lay
with corpses in my lime-pit
begging them answer,
then scratched their charms
in the oak's-skin under
the glow of Orlam.

Ira, you seer, you
sleepwalker, I see you
stumbling in outsized boots
through the wrong era
cradling the pale blue
sick-bowl of childhood.

Yet you shall meet *Him*,
the eternally bleeding Soldier.
You – a shepherdess who cannot
whistle, who only ever saw
one for sorrow, a not-girl,
not-boy. Bride of his Word.

Oh that I were . . . – a children's rhyme; *a shepherdess who cannot / whistle*
– refers to the song 'Whistle, Daughter, Whistle': 'Whistle, daughter,
whistle, / And you shall have a sheep. / Mother, I cannot whistle, /
Neither can I sleep. / / Whistle, daughter, whistle, / And you shall have
a cow. / Mother I cannot whistle, / Neither know I how. / / Whistle,
daughter, whistle, / And you shall a have a man. / Mother, I cannot
whistle, / But I'll do the best I can'; *Jew's ears* – a type of fungus; *The
Red Post* – UNDERWHELEM'S hanging post; *one for sorrow* – from
the child rhyme about magpies – 'one for sorrow, two for joy . . .'

A Premonition
Gore Woods

Difficult month that woke the alder
and woke the winds that whelmed
the daffodils and roses.

All the spiders reconvened
and earth firmed with bluebell leaves.
The elder tree spored his reek.

Gore Woods grew with stitchwort,
crane's bill, dove's foot
and dainty wood sorrel.

I smuggled silky wood-pigeon eggs
and thrush-blues from the larch,
until a mole's tiny fairy hand

lured me from my search
and waved me towards the shadows.
So I listened long in the bole of the ash

and heard the world turning
and as the magpie foretold
my own ghost-child a-nearing.

*

A Vorehearing

Gore Woods

Mazzerdy month that woke the aller
and woke the winds that whelmed
the yollerheads and roses.

Wevvet queens reconvened
and eth firmed with greygle leaves.
God's stinking tree a'spored 'es reek.

Gorey growed with stitchwort,
crane's bill, dove's foot
and dainty goocoo's bread.

I smuggled creezey culver eggs
and drush-blues from the larch,
till a want's tiny veäry hand

lured me from my sarch
and waved me t'wards the shadows.
So I lowsened long in the bole of the aish

and heard the wordle turning
and as the chattermag voretold
my soonere-child a'nearing.

*

O wildest, wildest wood
Of goodness and not good

Your darkness bowered above
Illumined only love

You met my black and white
My wrong-song and my right

By truth of axe and blade
Receive your shepherd maid

With tenderness at last
My lonesomeness is past

In fettered realm no more
I'll wander free in Gore

And shall walk clearly on
To where my king has gone

O wildest, wildest wood
Of goodness and not good

Your darkness bowered above
Illumined only love

You met my black and white
My wrong-song and my right

By truth of axe and blade
Receive your shepherd maid

With tenderness at last
My lwonesomness is past

In fettered realm no more
I'll vokket free in Gore

And shall walk clearly on
To where my king has gone

Wyman-Elvis

Forever bleeding
On a bed
Of mullein.
Kneel before him,
Faithful friend.
Consecrate
The throat-cut man.

Wyman-Elvis

Forever bleeding
On a bed
Of mullein.
Kneel before him,
Faithful friend.
Consecrate
The throat-cut man.

Wyman — warrior; *Elvis* — all-wise

John Forsey

His door was a board of smart-ply
and the windows polythene and masking-tape.

He lived by the entry to Gore Woods —
a bolted, five-bar, wooden gate.

I'd try to scoot down the track unseen
to spy on Forsey through the trees:

ragwort and bindweed in his garden,
Mrs. Forsey cooing into a pram of firewood,

Get in woman! from his tool shed
before spitting on his palm and turning his back

to polish something till he worked up a sweat.
He'd curse over the hedge

knowing I was there
that whole hallucinate summer

then one hazy morning
I crept past the empty garden

and waited for hours on my hands and knees
but saw nothing till I stood to leave:

Forsey in the clearing, watching me
with an axe, his corduroys below his knees

John Forsey

His door was a board of smart-ply
and the windows polythene and masking-tape.

He lived by the entry to Gore Woods —
a bolted, five-bar, wooden gate.

I'd try to scote down the track unseen
to spy on Forsey through the trees:

ragwort and bindweed in his garden,
Mrs. Forsey cooing into a pram of firewood,

Get in woman! from his tool shed
before spitting on his palm and turning his back

to polish something till he worked up a zweat.
He'd curse over the hedge

knowing I was there
that whole hallucinate summer

then one smoored morning
I crept past the empty garden

and waited for hours on my hands and knees
but saw nothing till I stood to leave:

Forsey in the clearing, watching me
with an axe, his corduroys below his knees

his lank hand kneading at his groin,
his Devil's-Cock throbbing.

He's cursing as I run
and leave the gate swinging open.

his lank hand kneading at his groin
his Ooser-Rod throbbing.

He's cursing as I run
and leave the gate swinging open.

Forsey – dweller by a furze-covered enclosure

A Badder Charm

I despise my brother's friend
So side with hatred till my end
For him, that boy that none can see.
My brother chose him over me.

I'll bleed myself into a brew
With spit of toad and ear of Jew
And charge my charm with ripening cruel,
I shall not be the spurnéd fool.

Come you spirits, sex me here!
I am the weird world's overseer!
Rail, you rooks, till you are hoarse –
Ira's evil intercourse!

I'll scratch my hatred like a scab
Till my rivals lie below the crab-
apple, eyes and guts all splayed –
The lamb-christ's sacrifice repaid.

A Badder Charm

I despise my brother's friend
An' hold wi' hatred till my end
For him, that boy that none can see.
My brother chose him over me.

I'll bleed myself into a brew
Wi' spet o' twoad and ear o' Jew
An' charge my charm wi' comely cruel,
I shatten be the spurnéd fool.

Come you spirits, sex I here!
Auverlook I allum weird!
Rail, you rooks, till you are hoarse –
Ira's evil intercourse!

Pick at hate as 'twere a scab
Till my usurpers 'neath the grab
Wi' eyes out-pecked an' gut-strings splayed;
The lamb-christ's sacrifice repaid.

Sly and stealthy I shall be
To see him not and not to see,
And now my kinder part has died
I'll end my hate at Never's Tide.

Undercreepen I shall be
To see him not and not to see,
An' now my kinder part has died
I'll end my hate at Never's Tide.

Come you spirits . . . – Lady Macbeth, 'The raven himself is hoarse / That croaks the fatal entrance of Duncan / Under my battlements. Come, you spirits / That tend on mortal thoughts, unsex me here, / And fill me from the crown to the toe topful / Of direst cruelty!' – *Macbeth*, Act 1, scene 5, 38–43; *Never's Tide* – a tide that never comes like 'the Greek Calends'

Round about, round about,
Maggoty pie;
My father loves good ale . . .

Drunk

The ewes have sodden rumps that smell like death.
We blowfly-dip in March against breech-strike.
The legless worms ascend the diazinon

as Chalmers, fortified by whiskey,
flogs the eldest ewe's bonce with a crook.
Her winker pops out, bounces on its rope.

Chalmers-Adam exits without guilt
the wall-eyed, blue-merle border at his heel.
Contaminated, Ira makes an oath:

I plant a crooked nail
on father-Chalmers's trail
towards The Golden Fleece
I plant a crooked nail

Round about, round about,
Maggoty pie;
My father loves good ale . . .

Maggoty

The ewes have sodden rumps that smell like death.
We blowfly-dip in March against breech-strike.
The legless worms ascend the diazinon

as Chalmers, fortified by whiskey,
flogs the eldest ewe's bonce with a crook.
Her winker pops out, bounces on its rope.

Chalmers-Adam exits without guilt
the wall-eyed, blue-merle border at his heel.
Contaminated, Ira makes an oath:

I plant a crooked nail
on father-Chalmers's trail
towards The Golden Fleece
I plant a crooked nail

Round about, round about . . . – children's rhyme; *breech-strike* –
a type of fly-strike in sheep; *blue-merle border* – breed of Collie dog

The Bowditches of Dogwell

Here the children
of UNDERWHELEM
were set-down
to be babysat

for three pounds a night.
At the front gate
brambles so high
we were led round the back

past a wood-stack, an axe
and The Red Shed.
The nursery room
at the top of the stairs

so cold in winter
that ice-webs would
knit themselves inside
the windows.

All night rats ran
in the attic.
Floorboards creaking
on the landing

then not.
Fingers of Fudge
in the front room;
Emery's armchair,

The Bowditches of Dogwell

Here the children
of UNDERWHELEM
were set-down
to be over-watched

for three pounds a night.
At the front gate
brembles so high
we were led round the back

past a wood-stack, an axe
and The Red Shed.
The nursy room
at the top of the stairs

so cold in winter
that ice wevvets would
knit themselves inside
the windows.

All night rats ran
in the parlour-sky.
Floorboards screaking
on the landing

then not.
Fingers of Fudge
in the front room;
Emery's armchair,

kisses from *Father*;
Father soft breathing
in your ear, *In peace
without fight*;

the corn baby
swinging from a rafter
in the draught from
the porch door.

kisses from *Father*;
Father soft breathing
in your ear, *In pes*
without vyhte;

the corn baby
swinging from a rafter
in the draught from
the hangen door.

Bowditch – 'above the ditch'; *The Red Shed* – The Bowditches' garden
shed; *In pes without vyhte* – 'in peace without fight', from a song from the
fourteenth century; *corn baby* – the last cut of the corn at harvest time
symbolised the 'spirit of the corn' and was tied into an animal or dolly
shape, 'corn dollies' or 'kern babies'. It was kept throughout the year for
luck and sometimes ploughed back into the ground when the first furrow
was cut on Plough Monday to ensure the fertility of that year's crop

Orlam Tells His Story

Loosed from the socket of sickly, black Mallory,
freed by the rooks of Blaggoty Knowle,
my jellied orb rolled Eleven Acres
furled with fleece and mud and bark
and trailing my yellow optic nerve
to wheel me in to the empty girl
whose little finger had suckled
my frail lamb.

I, Orlam, oracle of UNDERWHELEM,
shall keep her from the Forsey-Ooser jism,
from the corked wrath of Chalmers-Adam,
from fleece-fingered Aaron-Unwin,
from The-Red-Shed-sexer Dogger-Emerson,
and guide her to her scarlet bridegroom.

Orlam Tells His Story

Loosed from the socket of sickly, black Mallory,
freed by the rooks of Blaggoty Knowle,
my jellied orb rolled Eleven Acres
furled with fleece and mud and scroff
and trailing my yellow optic nerve
to wheel me in to the gawly girl
whose little finger had suckled
my frail lamb.

I, Orlam, oracle of UNDERWHELEM,
shall keep her from the Forsey-Ooser jism,
from the corked wrath of Chalmers-Adam,
from fleece-fingered Aaron-Unwin,
from The-Red-Shed-sexer Dogger-Emerson,
and guide her to her scarlet bridegroom.

Eleven Acres — a field in UNDERWHELEM

APRIL

Ira weaves a song about growing up in Hook House and on Hook Farm, and how father Chalmers fell in the sheep dip. We have lunch with Chalmers and consider his wall-eyed, blue merle Border Collie. Back in Gore Woods, Ira's tender love for Wyman-Elvis deepens. We enter Dogwell Cottage to better meet the Bowditches.

Things I Found in Gore Woods: April 1st

A robin's nest,
wind-wrecked
on the rotting leaf-bed.
Stole an egg
with crooked little fingers.

Things I Found in Gore Woods: April 1st

A reddick's nest,
wind-wrecked
on the rotting leaf-bed.
Stole an egg
with crooked little fingers.

crooked little fingers – children would be warned that if they ever stole an egg from a robin's nest, their little fingers would grow crooked

Cobweb

See a hand reach from a cot
In a one-time butcher's shop.
   Wake and weep,
   Count to sleep
An attic room of mice's feet.

Now she crawls across the floor.
Hark a single magpie's caw.
   See her rise,
   Seer's eyes,
Noon she'll hear the cockerel-cries.

Wednesday's child of horrid glee.
Heiress of grim memory.
   Through the hall
   Ghosties call.
Roaches scraping in the walls.

Kitchen cold as seven knives,
There she looms with augur's eyes.
   Mother-not.
   Father-sot.
Scrag-end hogget in the pot.

Flee The House of Hooks unfed,
Stomp around the garden shed.
   Cobweb maps,
   Scythes and sacks,
Playthings in The House of Traps.

Wevvet

See a hand reach from a cot
In a one-time butcher's shop.
   Wake and weep,
   Count to sleep
A parlour-sky of meeces' feet.

Now she crawls across the flags.
Hark a single chattermag.
   Up she grows,
   Seer's glow,
Noon she'll hear the cockerel crow.

Wednesday's child of horrid glee.
Heiress of grim memory.
   Through the hall
   Sooneres call.
Black-bobs scrooping in the walls.

Kitchen cold as zebm knives,
There she looms with heissen eyes.
   Mother-not.
   Father-sot.
Scrag-end hogget in the pot.

Flee The House of Hooks unfed,
Stumpy round the garden shed.
   Wevvet maps,
   Zives and zacks,
Playthings in The House of Traps.

In the cowshed on all fours
With the wethers licking salt.
    Eye to eye.
    Girl or boy?
Sheep don't care and nor do I.

Cemetery for little things,
Fur or feather found-e-lings.
    Disinterred
    Talk to her
UNDERWHELEM's furthermore.

Riddle river, coupling snake,
Ira's ankle, Adam's nape.
    Stones and leaves.
    Mysteries.
Shepherd girl to naked Eve.

Shit-faced path to The Golden Fleece.
Cast the murderous masterpiece:
    Lick a snail,
    Bury nail,
Wait for father's leg to fail.

Scribbling in the boarded barn,
Fungus-tongue and ringworm arm.
    Is that she?
    Is it me?
Am I friend or enemy?

In the hobble on all fours
With the wethers, licking salt.
   Eye to eye.
   Girl or boy?
Sheep don't care and nor do I.

Bwoneyard hwome for little things,
Fur or feather found-e-lings.
   Disinterred
   Talk to her
UNDERWHELEM's furthermore.

Riddle river, coupling snake,
Ira's ankle, Adam's nape.
   Stones and leaves.
   Mysteries.
Shepherd girl to naked Eve.

Shit-faced path to The Golden Fleece.
Cast the murderous masterpiece:
   Lick a snail,
   Grave a nail,
Wait for father's leg to fail.

Scratching in the boarded barn,
Orfy tongue and ringworm arm.
   Is that she?
   Is it me?
Am I friend or enemy?

Eye the sheep dip from beneath.
Filthy visions hatch and seethe –
   Maggots bloat,
   Father floats:
Bad meat in an overcoat.

Up The Fag Hole, down the lane,
Sucking hard for killer Kane –
   Favours hes,
   On their knees
Invisible as anus grease.

Woodland cobweb, rest in peace.
Spectres, animas and beasts
   Live and die,
   Ossify,
Fixed beneath the giant Eye.

Eye the sheep dip netherwise.
Vilthy visions hatch and rise –
   Maggots bloat,
   Father floats:
Cag-mag in an overcoat.

Up The Fag Hole, down the lane,
Sucking hard for killer Kane –
   Favours hes,
   On their knees
Invisible as anus greaze.

Woodland wevvet, rest in peace.
Spectres, animas and beasts
   Live and die,
   Ossify,
Fixed beneath the giant Eye.

The House of Hooks – The Rawles' family home, Hook House;
noon she'll hear the cockerel crow – one of the worst omens is to
hear a cock crowing at midday; *The House of Traps* – the garden
shed; *Fag Hole* – place to hide and smoke; mouth, anus

Lunch

I creep an awkward circle
around his shepherd's coat
tangled on its hook
beside the boot-room door.

And walk in terrified
with my little tongue caught
in my trap.

At the table-trough
Chalmers's face is ruddy
from the fury between
his huge sideburns.

Lunch ties a knot
in my innards.
Please sir, can I have no more?

Nammet

I creep a cammish circle
around 'es leather scrip
caddled on its hook
aside the hangen door.

An' enter I afeard
with little red rag trapped
in my crooked gap.

At the sarring table
Chalmers's face is ruddled
from veag 'tween
'es mutton chops.

Nammet ties a knot
in my inwards.
Pleaze zir, can I have no more?

The Wall-Eyed, Blue Merle Border

was the last whelp of a bad batch
bought from Doug Leathermewell.

It never had a name and was chained
to the hog oiler when not at Chalmers's heel.

Mad in the summer heat it would curl its lip
and show its fangs, with its back hairs stiffened.

It flashed its eye of blue, grey and brown
and whirled me down into a nether chamber;

I met my saviour in the shade.
I crossed the Riddle river.
I covered every curse of hate
With tender love forever.

The Wall-Eyed, Blue Merle Border

was the last whelp of a bad batch
bought from Doug Leathermewell.

It never had a name and was chained
to the hog oiler when not at Chalmers's heel.

Mad in the summer heat it would curl its lip
and show its fangs, with back hairs all a'stiver.

It flashed its eye of blue, grey and brown
and whirled me down into a nether chamber;

I met my saviour in the shade.
I crossed the Riddle river.
I healéd every haze of hate
With tender love forever.

wall eyed – heterochromia, when a dog has one blue eye and one brown or amber eye (also known as 'ghost eyes'; it has been said that such dogs can see both heaven and earth, but are not to be trusted); *blue merle* – the merle gene creates mottled patches of colour in a solid or piebald coat, blue or odd-coloured eyes, and can affect skin pigment as well; *hog oiler* – a mechanical device employed on farms to be used by hogs to provide relief from insects and offer skin protection. Hogs seeking relief would rub up against a wheel (or cylinder) causing it to rotate and dispense oil onto their bodies

Twigs

Four

Where the bee sucks there fuck I
In a cowslip's bell I lie
Where the flea sucks there fuck I
In a cowslip's head I die

Twiddicks

Vower

Where the bee sucks there vuck I
In a crewel's bell I lie
Where the vlee sucks there vuck I
In a holrod's head I die

Lonesome Tonight

Gore Woods

Hark the greening of the earth
Curly ferns yet to uncurl
Hark the singing of the birds
Girl is yearning to un-girl

Beech and alder, oak and birch,
Beetle, tadpole, squirrel's drey
Willow, aspen, elder, larch,
Soldier-King on Maundy day

In her satchel, Pepsi fizz,
Peanut-and-banana crusts
For this man her shepherd is.
Parts her bready-lips of love:

Are you Elvis? Are you God?
Jesus sent to win my trust?
Love Me Tender, *are his words,*
As I have loved you, so you must . . .

Thrice she draws her lips to kiss
Mouthing for his mouth in vain
Thrice her lonesome kisses miss,
My love, will you come back again?

Lwonesome Tonight

Gore Woods

Hark the greening of the eth
Curl-ed ferns yet to uncurl
Hark the zingen of the birds
Gurrel yearns yet to un-gurrel

Beech and aller, woak and birch,
Biddle, bull-head, squirrel's drey
Willow, aspen, elder, larch,
Soldier-King on Maundy day

In her satchel, Pepsi fizz,
Peanut-and-banana crusts
For this man her shepherd is.
Parts her bready-lips of love:

Are you Elvis? Are you God?
Jesus sent to win my trust?
Love Me Tender, *are his words,*
As I have loved you, so you must . . .

Thrice she draws her lips to kiss
Mouthing for his mouth in vain
Thrice her lwonesome kisses miss,
My love, will you come back again?

'As I have loved you, so you must love one another.' – John 13:34;
'Is your heart filled with pain / Shall I come back again? / Tell me
dear, are you lonesome tonight?' – from 'Are You Lonesome Tonight?'

Emery Bowditch

Once *ruler of work*, he opened the bellies
of pregnant ewes and sealed fox holes
beneath a Blaggot's Moon.

He stopped the life of rabbit and pheasant
between thumb and finger, and gently whispered
tender love to ease them.

Now *Father* of Dogwell dwindles
in a rotten armchair.
Father's nose drips and he wants kisses;

cold snot in the child's mouth
as the district nurse undresses
his weeping ulcers.

Emery Bowditch

Once *ruler of work*, he opened the bellies
of pregnant ewes and sealed fox holes
beneath a Blaggot's Moon.

He let life between thumb and finger
of bunker and longtail and gently whispered
tender love to ease them.

Now *Father* of Dogwell dwindles
in a rafty armchair.
Father's nose drips and he wants kisses;

cold snot in the child's mouth
as the district nurse undresses
his weeping ulcers.

Emery – 'ruler of work/labour'; *Bowditch* – 'above the ditch'; Blaggot's
Moon – UNDERWHELEM's full moon in October, named for a wealthy
landowner, Thomas Blaggot, who according to UNDERWHELEM
folklore is buried upright on his horse in Gore Woods

Myra Bowditch

Mild *Mother* of Dogwell;
hoarder of Netherland Dwarfs;
damp bedstraw-stinker.

Babysit-woman for infants abandoned,
she carries comforts in her apron
of Walnut Whips and Curly Wurly.

Her hair is a wisp of dandelion seeds;
her cheeks are crimson cobwebs;
her eyes are blue butterflies

forever weepy. See her teeter
to the inn with her Safeway bag
in a drinky dream. See her swoon

as the cade lambs suck her milky fingers,
as weasels ooze beneath her palms,
as rabbits pant in her cradling arms.

Myra Bowditch

Mild *Mother* of Dogwell;
hoarder of Netherland Dwarfs;
dank bedstraw-raker.

Over-watch woman for bantlings bandoned,
she carries comforts in her apron
of Walnut Whips and Curly Wurly.

Her hair is a wisp of piss-a-bed seed;
her cheeks are crimson wevvets;
her eyes are blue vlutterbies

forever weepy. See her teeter
to the inn with her Safeway bag
in a fleecy dream. See her zweem

as the orphans suck her milchi fingers,
as veäres peaze beneath her palms,
as bunkers pank in her cradling arms.

Myra – 'sweet-smelling oil'; *Netherland Dwarf* – breed of rabbit

Emerson-Dogger Bowditch

Sire of The Red Shed;
only-child above the ditch;
monster-cocked grown son, still sewn

into a goose-grease vest for winter.
Lanky, pock-marked, fugly,
who buffs his knee-naps, hand-leathers

and GT Fantic Chopper.
Dogger of the lay-by;
sexer of four gloomy daughters.

Creaker of floorboards
on the baby-sit landing.
Creepy-crooner at the nursery door;

Four corners to your bed,
Four angels all a-spread;
One at head and one at feet,

And two to keep your soul asleep.

Emerson-Dogger Bowditch

Rudger of The Red Shed;
only-child above the ditch;
brushen-knogged grown son, still sewn

into a goose-grease vest for winter.
Speare, pock-fretten, munter,
who buffs his knee-naps, hand-leathers

and GT Fantic Chopper.
Dogger of the lay-by;
sexer of four dungy daughters.

Creaker of floorboards
on the over-watch landing.
Crimsy-crooner at the nursy door;

Vow'r carners to your bed,
Vow'r aangels all a-spread;
Oone at head an' oone at veet,

An' two to keep your soul asleep.

Emerson – 'son of Emery'; *goose-grease vest* – goose grease was
considered a panacea, and a child might be sewn into a goose-
grease vest in winter as a protection against chest ailments; *knee-
naps & hand-leathers* – thatcher's tools; *GT Fantic Chopper* – type of
moped; *Vow'r carners . . .* – four corners, West Country bed charm

MAY

Ira takes us deeper into Gore Woods where she has many questions for the soldier-ghosts of The Ransham Rebellion about their comrade, Wyman-Elvis. We praise the May Tree and The Eye of The Lamb. May is the month of the unsexing of Ira in The Red Shed by Emerson-Dogger Bowditch. Ira then makes a ravished rhyme at the month's end.

Twigs
Five

Wild arum, cuckoopint
Hooded hairy priest
Up and down his purple pole
Basting with the beast

Twiddicks

Vive

Wild arum, goocoo pint
Hooded hairy priest
Up and down 'es purple pole
Basting with the beast

Two bodies have I,
Though both joined in one
The stiller I stand,
The faster I run

In the Woods

The sirens of Gore
    were oak, ash and hawthorn
At the year's sunset
    I caught their souls falling

I gathered the messages
    laced through the grouse pen
by wandering ghosts
    my sisters and brothers

and gave myself up
    to The Lamb and The Soldier
far from Hook House
    its draughts and its yammer.

Always so serious
    gloomy and woeful
but mine were the ash-trees'
    moaning and tumble

Two bodies have I,
Though both joined in one
The stiller I stand,
The faster I run

In the Woods

The sirens of Gore
    were oak, ash and hawthorn
At the year's sunset
    I caught their souls falling

I gathered the messages
    laced through the grouse pen
by wandering sooneres
    my sisters and brothers

and gave myself up
    to The Lamb and The Soldier
far from Hook House
    and its draty and blether.

Always so serious
    twanketen, woeful
but mine were the aishy trees'
    hustle and tumble

and starling swarms, entrails
and greeny jewelled beetles
who gave me their charms
and their horrible omens.

Back on the school bus
the farm boys eat bogies
taunting me, *Pox-girl*
sheep s/himmer, minger.

I scratch in the window-mist
INBREDS and *DEATHBEDS*.
Bad things will happen
to them in the tool sheds.

and starling swarms, entrails
    and greeny jewelled beetles
who gave me their charms
    and their horrible heissens.

Back on the school bus
    the farm boys eat bogies
girding me, *Orf-gurrel*
    sheep shimmer, minger.

I scratch in the wilder-mist
    INBREDS and *DEATHBEDS.*
Bad things will happen
    to them in the tool sheds.

orf – a viral form of pustular dermatitis found
in sheep, and communicable to humans

Questions for The Red Post Ghosts
seeking Wyman-Elvis

Who knows his name?
The ghostie John Penne.

Who knows his age?
The ghost Evan Page.

Who knows his kin?
The ghost Eli King.

One of twin-born,
Says ghost William Fawn.

Who saw him pray?
The ghost Jesse Gray.

Who heard him beg?
The ghostie Sam Legg.

Who caught his tears?
The ghost Isaac Steer.

Who saw him stabbed?
The ghostie Tom Crabb.

Who watched him hung?
The ghost Amos Stone.

Questions for The Red Post Sooneres

seeking Wyman-Elvis

Who knows his name?
The ghostie John Penne.

Who knows his age?
The ghost Evan Page.

Who knows his kin?
The ghost Eli King.

One of twin-born,
Says ghost William Fawn.

Who saw him pray?
The ghost Jesse Gray.

Who heard him beg?
The ghostie Sam Legg.

Who caught his tears?
The ghost Isaac Steer.

Who saw him stabbed?
The ghostie Tom Crabb.

Who watched him hung?
The ghost Amos Stone.

Who saw him drawn?
The ghostie Job Thorne.

Who cut him down?
The ghost Wheelhouse Brown.

Who heard his song?
The ghost Robert Young.

Who bears his Word?
A little shep-herd.

Who saw him drawn?
The ghostie Job Thorne.

Who cut him down?
The ghost Wheelhouse Brown.

Who heard his song?
The ghost Robert Young.

Who bears his Word?
A little shep-herd.

Carving on the May Tree

In my heart there is room
for good to be born,
as long as a sprig of you
's left to be worn.

Scratching on the May Tree

In my heart there is room
for good to be born,
as long as a sprig of you
's left to be worn.

Seems to Me

Sodden sheep went blaring
across Eleven Acres

as belling from the churchyard
tangled round the orchard

the scarlet sky a-warning
as wailing from the kitchen

from baby girl dread-filled
abandoned on a breadboard

This not-girl grew to searching
for the other half of something

and waded Riddle river
with cow-bones and dead leaves

her fingernails a-ripped
from hauling clay-filled fists

out of the Riddle's edges
for pots with happy voices

Seem an I

Bedraggled angels blethered
across Eleven Acres

as belling from the bwoneyard
a-rangled round the archet

the scarlet sky a-warning
as wailing from the kitchen

from baby gurrel dread-fulled
lone-left on a breadboard

This not-girl growed to sarching
for the other half of something

and waded Riddle river
with hummock-bones and tree-tears

her fingernails a-ripped
from hauling clay-filled fists

out of the Riddle's edges
for pots with happy voices

Swollen tonsils croaking
for The Lamb already taken

and lost beloved brother
once her tightest buddy

consumed by melancholy
that's only eased by writing

wisp-words slim as thistles,
or a dying chicken's whistles

till in the vaulted barn
queer-lit by dusky sun

she knew herself a vessel
fit for a different world

where footsteps must be lone
and barefoot upon stones

and the northwind's ever-host
gives edges to the ghosts

Waxen crundels croaking
for The Lamb already taken

and lost beloved brother
once thickest inkle weaver

conzum-ed with twanketen
that's only eased by scratching

wisp-words slim as thistles,
or a sickly chicken's whistles

till in the vaulted barn
queer-lit by dummet zun

she knew herself a vessel
fit for a different wordle

where footsteps must be lwone
and barefoot upon stones

and the northwind's ever-host
gives edges to the ghosts

Seems to me a childhood
of poisoned blood and wormwood

of not-friends running nowhere
of fog a-veiling elsewhere

of mother's voice not calling
of corrugated iron

of magpie-croaks and whiskey
of yearling ewes and drinky

and joy I could not reap

and joy I could not reap

Seem an I a childhood
of quartere'il and wormwood

of not-friends running nowhere
of vog a-veiling elsewhere

of mother's voice not calling
of corrugated iron

of devil's birds and whiskey
of chilver hogs and fleecy

and nuts I could not reapy

and nuts I could not reapy

The Eye of The Lamb

Great Ink pasture
Field of longing
Lovely coffin

The Eye of The Lamb

Great Ink grotten
Leaze of longing
Lovesome coffin

Great Ink – a rectangular field in UNDERWHELEM

Bumping in The Red Shed

May 30th

Emerson and empty girl
are here to stroke the weasels.
Emerson in hand-leathers
with two thumbs poking clear.

He hunkers on a milking stool,
pulls girl on his lap,
and shoos a sort of nursing song
from panting little trap.

Ride away, ride away,
Johnny shall ride . . .
Ride away, ride away
Johnny's inside . . .

Hedge-gloves hanging from a nail
begin to slow-hand-clap
as Emerson bumps empty girl
to OVERWHELEM and back.

*

Once she was a velvet bud
cocooned in evermore,
but now she seeps all milky
on a manky forest floor.

Bumping in The Red Shed
May 30th

Emerson and gawly gurrel
are here to stroke the veäres.
Emerson in hand-leathers
wi' thumbles poking clear.

He croopies on a milking stool,
pulls gurrel on his lap,
and shoos a sort of nursy song
from panking little gap.

Ride away, ride away,
Johnny shall ride . . .
Ride away, ride away
Johnny's inside . . .

Codgloves hanging from a nail
begin to slow-hand-clap
as Emerson bumps gawly-gurrel
to OVERWHELEM and back.

*

Once she was a velvet bud
cocooned in evermore,
but now she seeps all milchi
on a furby forest floor.

Once she was a crooked rhyme
and ever-free to roam,
but now she's cold-at-supper-time
and'll nevermore go home.

Once she was a bandy-rhyme
and ever-free to roam,
but now she's cold-at-supper-time
and'll nevermore go hwome.

Ride away . . . – from the children's rhyme, 'Ride away, ride away, / Johnny shall ride, / He shall have a pussy cat / Tied to one side; / He shall have a little dog / Tied to the other, / And Johnny shall ride / To see his grandmother'; *milchi* – 'Thri-milchi' was the Anglo-Saxon name for May as cows could be milked three times a day because of the lush grass

Ira on the Nether-edge

Gore Woods

March will search, April will try,
May will tell if you'll live or die.

Ravished 'neath the milky moon
barefoot with the sylvan
rambling to a ghostie's tune
sheathed in veils of evening

buds a-break and milky seeps
heady in the meadows
chalky children on the steep
baskets full of shadows

nightjar spins a rattle song
air's an upturned ocean
swift's an axe hurled in the gloam
splits the Riddle open

poisoned blood takes a wife:
ewe-lamb meets her maker
as the grindstone turns the knife
over Eleven Acres

now it looks it almost sounds
world circles wider
with the silence upside down
horse atop the rider

Ira on the Nether-edge

Gore Woods

March 'ull sarch, Eäpril 'ull try,
Mäy 'ull tell if you'll live or die.

Ravished 'neath the milchi moon
barefoot with the sylvan
owling to a soonere's tuen
sheathed in veils of evemen

buds a-break and milchi seeps
heady in the meadows
chalky children on the steep
baskets full of shadows

gapmouth spins a rattle song
air's an upturned ocean
swift's an axe hurled in the gloam
splits the Riddle open

quaterevil takes a wife:
chilver meets her maker
as the grindstone turns the knife
o'er Eleven Acres

now it looks it almost zounds
wordle zircles wider
with the silence upside down
horse atop the rider

girl-boys in the forest find
figs of foul freedom
where the old you left behind
falls through nether-Eden

Some must watch, while some must sleep
so runs the world's way;
a not-girl scorchéd at the stake
a-births the end of May

femboys in the forest find
figs of foul freedom
where the old you left behind
valls through nether-Eden

Some must watch, while some must sleep
so runs the wordle's way;
a not-girl zweal-ed at the stake
a-births the end of May

March 'ull sarch . . . – an old saying about health and weather; 'For
some must watch, while some must sleep / So runs the world away' –
Hamlet; *a not-girl zweal-ed at the stake* – Joan of Arc, d. May 30th, 1431

June

June is the month of the soonere-children, the ghostly Ash-Wraiths who live in the grouse pen in Gore Woods. June is the month of swooning at midnight on Midsummer's Eve and of mother Lola's wandering. Ira sings of Kane-Jude the wonder-brother and a few of her very favourite things.

Grouse Pen

The disused hold seemed built
to take in the splintered souls
attending your steps: children of the dark places,
their lithesome wraiths skittering in the leaves –
and you, scuffing your boots
trying to conjure an invisible friend.

How could you have known then
that the offerings you left to entice them –
hawfinch eggs, lambs' tails, jars of spawn –
were grave goods to ease your own passing
beneath the canopy of ash,
whose leaves are still green when they fall.

Grouse Pen

The disused hold seemed built
to take in the spawly souls
attending your steps: children of the dark places
their litty wraiths skittering in the leaves –
and you, scuffing your boots
trying to conjure an invisible friend.

How could you have known then
that the offerings you left to entice them –
hawfinch eggs, lambs' tails, jars of spawn –
were grave goods to ease your own passing
beneath the canopy of ash,
whose leaves are still green when they fall.

Midsummer's Eve
Midnight, Gore Woods

As fires that burn Barnaby Bright
Praise longest day and shortest night

As chervil leans and lily seeps,
As spear-grass keens and mare's-tail sweeps
She stomps into the emerald gloam
Through horny gates to nether home;

A sylvan tomb for slaughtered kings,
An ashen womb for infant wings,
Air warm and damp, a-spored and rank,
The brook a-pulsing against her banks.

Here, sup the cream of wolfsbane milk,
Here, rub the heavenly hawk-moth silk.
Her lonesome soul at last a-freed
And met with shadows under the trees.

As fires that burn Barnaby Bright
Praise longest day and shortest night

Midsummer's Eve

Midnight, Gore Woods

As fires that burn Barnaby Bright
Praise longest day and shortest night

As eltroot leans and snake's-head seeps,
As foxtails keen and mare's-tail sweeps
She stumpies in the emerald gloam
Through horny gates to nether hwome;

A sylvan tomb for cleavéd kings,
An ashen womb for infant wings,
Air warm an' damp, a'spored an' rank,
The brook a-pulsing 'gainst her banks.

Here, sup the cream of wolfsbane milk,
Here, rub the heabmly hawk-moth silk.
Her lwonesome soul at last a-freed
And met with shadows 'neath the trees.

As fires that burn Barnaby Bright
Praise longest day and shortest night

Barnaby Bright – St Barnabas' Day (the longest day)

Elda-Mary Rawles

Soft skin, milky as the moon.
One crooked leg, a walking cane.
Toadstool thumbs all screwy grown.

Our Father's mammy. Blessed Lady
of belly-aches; brittle biscuits
and chitterling cakes.

Under earth at sixty-eight
when a clot clogged up her womb;
it swelled until our grandma's breath

flew from the corner of the room;
and then a strange and chilly song
cloaked the shaken groves of Gore:

Hush-a-bye, don't you cry,
a-gnashing at the empty gates
and skittering through the sycamore.

Elda-Mary Rawles

So't skin, milchi as the moon.
Oone bandy leg, a walking cane.
Twoad's meat thumbles, screwy grown.

Our Farter's mammy. Blessed Lady
of belly-aches; brickley biscuits,
and chetlens cakes.

Nether-ethed at zixty-aïght,
when a clot cagged in her crate
and plimmed until the peart o' gramm'er

vlit from the carner of the chammer;
and then a rum, shram song
smoored the shockled groves of Gore:

Hush-a-bye, don't you cry,
gnanging at the gawly geates
and skeating through the sycamore.

Elda – 'old and wise protector'; *Mary* – 'beloved lady, sea
of bitterness'; *Hush-a-bye, don't you cry* – taken from a song
('Go to sleep, my little P–'), often sung innocently as a lullaby
to Dorset children in the 1970s by the older generation

Lola in My Bedroom

Nights in white satin
Always this song
Nearby but not there
Rightfully wrong

Holding a letter
Not meant to send
Mother of *Never-*
Reaching the end

Lola in My Night Chammer

Nights in white satin
Always this song
Nearen but not there
Rightfully wrong

Holding a letter
Not meant to send
Mother of *Never-*
Reaching the end

Nights in White Satin . . . Never reaching
the end – a song by the Moody Blues

Kane-Jude Rawles

Lovely brother, child-god,
Master of *The Wonder Rod!*
Your face immaculate and kind.
Mine a mask I crouch behind.

I the girl/boy lamb who scoffs
Dumpy from the under-trough;
You the best-boy record-breaker,
Honoured heir of Every Acre.

We were besties to the end
Until you bred an inward friend
Who banished me to never-sleep
In search of love from ghosts and sheep.

Solitary till my death
I'll ever-roam the under-earth
A-snarled with hate, a-smeared with grief,
Suspicion etched in every leaf.

Kane-Jude Rawles

Lovesome brother, child-god,
Master of *The Wonder Rod!*
Your face immaculate and kind.
Mine a mask I croop behind.

I the clodgy chilver/wether
Scoffing from a trough of nether;
You the best-boy record-breaker,
Honoured heir of Every Acre.

We were inkles to the end
Until you bred an inward friend
Who banished me to never-sleep
In search of love from ghosts and sheep.

Solitary till my death
I'll ever-roam the nether-eth
A'harled with hate, a'smamed with grief,
Suspicion scratched in every leaf.

Kane – 'honour, a boy's name'; *Jude* – 'praised'; *The Wonder Rod* – penis

Twigs

Six

Foxy little Ira,
randy reddened rump
Shifty little Ira,
saucy maggot stump

Twiddicks

Zix

Undercreepen Ira,
randy ruddled rump
Undercreepen Ira,
mandy maggot stump

ruddle – a red earth by which sheep are marked

My Favourite Things
Gore Woods

To be sung to the tune of 'My Favourite Things'

Nightjar a-scraping and ghost moth a-flapping
Brushing my face with ethereal satin
Numb in a swimmy dance on woozy wings
These are a few of my favourite things

Blackthorn and buttercup, cuckoo-pint's oozes
Speedwell and woundwort a-boasting their bruises
Feasting my way through some false morel rings
These are a few of my favourite things

Dragonfly, death-beetle, field-mouse and vole
Used rubber johnny – pink worm with a hole
Wetting my lips 'neath the feet of The King
These are a few of my favourite things

When the dog bites
When the wasp stings
When I'm feeling sad
I simply remember my favourite things
And then I don't feel so bad

Down in the quaking grass, feather-like silky
Laying against me like creamy on milky
Wetting my lips 'neath the feet of The King
These are a few of my favourite things

My Favourite Things

Gore Woods

To be sung to the tune of 'My Favourite Things'

Gapmouth a'scraping and ghost moth a'flappin'
Brushing my face with his thear-re-al satin
Numb in a zweemy-dance on woozy wings
These are a few of my favourite things

Gribble and giltcup and goocoo pint's oozes
Speedwell and woundwort a'boasting their bruises
Feasting my way through some false morel rings
These are a few of my favourite things

Ho's adder, death-biddle, moule and voley
Used rubber johnny – pink yis with a holey
Wetting my lips 'neath the feet of The King
These are a few of my favourite things

When the dog bites
When the wops stings
When I'm feeling sad
I simply remember my favourite things
And then I don't feel so bad

Wagwanton grasses, all feather-like silky
Laying against me like creamy on milky
Wetting my lips 'neath the feet of The King
These are a few of my favourite things

July

Ira dresses herself in white and goes to Wyman-Elvis to be Washed in the Blood of The Lamb. *We philosophise with the hedgerow and praise the ash trees. It's time for reaping. Ira makes a spell for father Chalmers and we hear how she managed to escape Hook House. Ira looks for mother Lola in the garden shed.*

Twigs

Seven

Leg for a bow
Wing for a string
Hear the frisky grasshopper
Sing, sing, sing!

Twiddicks

Zebm

Leg for a bow
Wing for a string
Hear the litty frog-hopper
Zing, zing, zing!

Washed in the Blood

Ira Sings

I have been to Elvis for his crimson shower
I am washed in the Blood of The Lamb
I swam in Sonny's socket till the milk turned sour
I am washed in the Blood of The Lamb

I am washed, (I am washed), in the blood, (in the blood),
In the soul-cleansing Blood of The Lamb
My wedding dress is spotless, it is white as wool
I am washed in the Blood of The Lamb

I am walking daily with the crucified
I am washed in the Blood of The Lamb
Ransham Dead a'whistling a-by my side,
I am washed in the Blood of The Lamb

I am washed, (I am washed), in the blood, (in the blood),
In the soul-cleansing Blood of The Lamb
My wedding dress is spotless, it is white as wool
I am washed in the Blood of The Lamb

Wyman-Elvis bleeding on my robes of white
I am washed in the Blood of The Lamb
Sonny's eye all-seeing through the day and night
I am washed in the Blood of The Lamb

Washed in the Blood

Ira Sings

I have been to Elvis for his crimson shower
I am washed in the Blood of The Lamb
I swam in Sonny's socket till the milk turned sour
I am washed in the Blood of The Lamb

I am washed, (I am washed), in the blood, (in the blood),
In the soul-cleansing Blood of The Lamb
My wedding dress is spotless, it is white as wool
I am washed in the Blood of The Lamb

I am walking daily with the crucified
I am washed in the Blood of The Lamb
Ransham Dead a'whistling a-by my side,
I am washed in the Blood of The Lamb

I am washed, (I am washed), in the blood, (in the blood),
In the soul-cleansing Blood of The Lamb
My wedding dress is spotless, it is white as wool
I am washed in the Blood of The Lamb

Wyman-Elvis bleeding on my robes of white
I am washed in the Blood of The Lamb
Sonny's eye all-seeing through the day and night
I am washed in the Blood of The Lamb

Sonny in the sedge grass with his head caved in
I am washed in the Blood of The Lamb
Crimson fountain flowing under Wyman's chin
I am washed in the Blood of The Lamb

Chalmers bleating Amen! *on the poison bed*
Forsey in a sack with antlers on his head
Aaron-Unwin's barnet soaked from white to red
Emerson-the-Sexer on his wrecked moped

I am washed, (I am washed), in the blood, (in the blood),
In the soul-cleansing Blood of The Lamb
My wedding dress is spotless, it is white as wool
I am washed in the Blood of The Lamb

Sonny in the zedgemocks with his head caved in
I am washed in the Blood of The Lamb
Crimson fountain flowing under Wyman's chin
I am washed in the Blood of The Lamb

Chalmers blethers Amen! *on the poison bed*
Forsey in a sack with antlers on his head
Aaron-Unwin's barnet soaked from white to red
Emerson-the-Sexer on his wrecked moped

I am washed, (I am washed), in the blood, (in the blood),
In the soul-cleansing Blood of The Lamb
My wedding dress is spotless, it is white as wool
I am washed in the Blood of The Lamb

'Are You Washed in the Blood of The Lamb' — a song by Elisha A. Hoffman

A Child's Question

Hail the hedgerow as it grows
Ask the hedgerow all it knows

Tell me who has licked the toad?
What is hidden 'neath the road?
Tell me quick as I was born
Quivering like a downy horn.

Hail the hedgerow as it grows
Ask the hedgerow all it knows

Who's inside The Devil's-Cock?
Horny devil? Goaty God?
What is God in earthly guise?
One or million giant eyes?

Hail the hedgerow as it grows
Ask the hedgerow all it knows

Will the dream of golden keys
Hanging in the high ash trees
Open empty gates to Death
Who hoards his answers in the earth?

A Child's Question

Hail the hedgerow as it grows
Ask the hedgerow all it knows

Tell me who has licked the twoad?
What is hidden 'neath the road?
Tell me quick as I was born
Whivering like a downy horn.

Hail the hedgerow as it grows
Ask the hedgerow all it knows

Who's inneath The Ooser-Rod?
Horny devil? Goaty God?
What is God in ethly guise?
One or mampus giant eyes?

Hail the hedgerow as it grows
Ask the hedgerow all it knows

Will the sweven's golden keys
Hanging in the aishy trees
Open gawly geates to Death
Who hoards 'es answers in the eth?

Ash

Venus of the Woods

S/hims and she-males
bent in the north wind
swooning saplings
milky in moonlight

velvet buds
as yet unopened
dropping their keys
high on carbon

friends to the rooks
redstarts and hawk-moth
friends to the phantoms
caught between stations

friends to sleepwalking
unsexed Ira
Wednesday's child
who weeps upon waking

Ash

Venus of the Woods

Shims and she-males
bent in the Boreas
swooning saplings
milky in moonlight

velvet buds
as yet unopened
dropping their keys
high on carbon

friends to the rooks
redstarts and hawk-moth
friends to the phantoms
caught between stations

friends to sleepwalking
unsexed Ira
Wednesday's child
who weeps upon waking

friends to the sheep-girl
with pox on her tongue
friends to the soldiers
pitch-boiled and hung

friends to the sheep-girl
with orf on her tongue
friends to the soldiers
pitch-boiled and hung

Venus of the Woods – the ash tree, for its graceful form and
beautiful foliage. The ash was credited with a range of protective
and healing properties, most frequently related to children.
Newborn babies were popularly given a teaspoon of ash sap

Reaping

Once a barley seed was sown.
All must be cut down once grown.

Men shall fall beneath the elm,
Under earthly overwhelm.

Free from flesh and free from blood,
All our shades flit to the wood.

Evening holds them in his gloam,
Chalky children take them home,

Merge them with the moss and leaves,
Conjure us to silent sheaves.

Reaping

Once a spileful seed was sown.
All must be cut down once grown.

Men shall vall beneath the elm,
Under ethly overwhelm.

Freen from fleshy, freen from bloods,
All our shades flit to the woods.

Evemen holds em in 'es gloam,
Chalky children take em hwome,

Merge em with the meesh, an' leaves,
Conjure us to silent sheaves.

Hanging Out with Chalmers

Do you recall how father Rawles
Would a-flash his wrinkly balls,
Furled with curly hair and warts,
Poking out his boxer shorts?

Dance a demon in the bog,
Curse his brown-and-blue-eyed dog,
Ruinate his porky sword,
Nail it to the flour board!

Hanging Out with Chalmers

Do you recall how father Rawles
Wouldst a'flash 'es wrinkly balls,
Furled with curdled hair and warts,
Poking out 'es boxer shorts?

Dance a demon in the bog,
Auverlook 'es wall-eyed dog,
Ruinate 'es porky-sword,
Nail it to the flour board!

The House of Hooks

Once I was a happy girl,
A curl upon my forehead;
I followed not my father's crook
But fled into the forest.

My father withered to a wart
Of yellow rage and poison.
His blue merle scratched outside the door
And howled, I am an orphan!

The House of Hooks

Once I was a happy girl,
A curdle on my forehead;
I followed not my father's crook
But fled into the forest.

My father withered to a wart
Of yoller pelt and poison.
His blue merle scratched outside the door
And howled, I am an orphan!

The House of Traps

Grave-earth hunger made her roam:
this shed became a holding room,
the doorway lit by two gas lamps.

I see it now: our father limps
towards the door, and bends to tip
into the hatch a plate of tup.

Inside, a bench of rusted cans,
shepherd's crooks and walking canes,
hack-saw blades and hogget shears.

I call to you over Never's Shires,
Mother! Lola! and try to feel
your ghostly breath, but I'm the fool.

Inmates now, we share this cell,
this unmet, lonesome, tangled soul.

The House of Traps

Ether-hunger made her roam:
this shed became a holding room,
the doorway lit by two gas lamps.

I see it now: our father limps
towards the door, and bends to tip
into the hatch a plate of tup.

Inside, a bench of rusted cans,
shepherd's crooks and walking canes,
hack-saw blades and hogget shears.

I call to you o'er Never's Shires,
Mother! Lola! and try to feel
your soonere breath, but I'm the fool.

Inmates now, we share this cell,
this unmet, lwonesome, rangling soul.

ether-hunger – the hunger for earth (eth)
sometimes felt by persons approaching death

August

It's the end of the summer holidays and the birds are leaving. Ira takes comfort from The Word of her saviour. We praise the thistle and address Ira's childhood nemesis, Aaron-Unwin White. Ira's sheep-farm upbringing prompts her to ask: just what is unnatural? We praise the sheep, and as childhood death comes ever closer, summer is over.

A Child's Question
End of the Summer Holidays

Starling swarms will soon be lorn.
Rooks tell stories 'cross the corn.
Cuckoo soon will his leave make.
Swifts abandon autumn's ache.
What says sparrow, thrush or dove?
Love Me Tender? Tender love?

Hear the grinding nightjar grieve.
Grief unknits my ravelled sleeve.
Death of summer, death of play,
Waxing night and dwindling day.
Help me sparrow, thrush and dove.
Love Me Tender. Tender love.

A Child's Question
End of the Summer Holidays

Starling swarms will soon be lorn.
Rooks tell stories 'cross the corn.
Goocoo soon will 'es leave make.
Swifts abandon autumn's ache.
What says dunnick, drush or dove?
Love Me Tender? Tender love?

Hear the grinding wheel-bird grieve.
Grief unknits my ravelled sleeve.
Death of zummer, death of play,
Waxing night and dwindling day.
Help me dunnick, drush and dove.
Love Me Tender. Tender love.

'Do you ask what the birds say? The Sparrow, the Dove, / The Linnet and Thrush say, "I love and I love!"' – 'Answer to a Child's Question', Samuel Taylor Coleridge; *unknits my ravelled sleeve* – 'Sleep that knits up the ravell'd sleeve of care, / The death of each day's life,' *Macbeth*, Act 2, Scene 2, 35

A Noiseless Noise
Gore Woods

Evening sent you stomping
through ripened barley, thorns and briers
that pierced the cauls of sleep.

Mizzle wet your hot brow
but couldn't balm your forsakenness
at the absence of birds

as cold moon comes curling
through reddening leaves.
UNDERWHELEM.

*

Know you every leaf
in these woods, every place
of good and not-good,

between sleep and wake
and bellyache, each path
uncovered and well-trodden.

*

Burnt embers. The end of summer.
Unravel the Riddle's tangled tongue
of tarnished silver —

A Noiseless Noise
Gore Woods

Evemen sent you trapesen
through ripened spiles, thorns and briers
that pierced the braims of sleep.

Drisk wet your hetful brow
but couldn' balm your bandon
at the absence of birds

as cold moon comes curdling
through reddenin' leaves.
UNDERWHELEM.

*

Know you every tree-tear
in these woods, every place
of good and not-good,

'tween sleep and wake
and bellyache, each path
unhealed and stumpied.

*

Charkened embers. The end of summer.
Reeve the Riddle's tardle tongue
of smirchéd silver —

Come away love and leave your wandering . . .

Just a noiseless noise,
just a hollow girl,
just a bogus boy –

Go home now, leave your wandering . . .

Stomp the fields of faces
to a chamber of not-sleep.
Count the ghoul moths trancing at your window.

Come away love and leave your wandering . . .

Just a noiseless noise,
just a gawly girl,
just a bogus boy —

Go home now, leave your wandering . . .

Trapes the fields of feasen
to a chammer of not-sleep.
Count the ghoul moths trancing at your window.

'And then there crept / A little noiseless noise among the leaves. / Born of the very sigh that silence leaves' — John Keats, 'I Stood Upon A Little Hill'

Things I Found in Gore Woods: August 10th

His barby thiefdom
from Greater Gore
to OVERWHELEM:
thistle, king
of nowhere's land.

Things I Found in Gore Woods: August 10th

His barby thiefdom
from Greater Gore
to OVERWHELEM:
thistle, king
of nowhere's land.

Aaron-Unwin White

Four-eyed coward, with palest skin
and hair like a cloud of up-sprayed spunk.

He swallows worms and woodlice,
wears ewe's-muff cologne and goat perfume.

A straddle-me-face farter. A Chinese-torturer.
Enlightened of god? Methinks not.

Aaron-Unwin White

Vower-eyed cowheart, wi' palest 'plexion
an' hair like a cloud of upsmitten spume.

'E swallows yis an' button-crawlers,
wears ewe's-muff cologne, an' goat perfume.

A straddle-me-face farter. A Chinese-torturer.
Enlightened of god? Methinks not.

Aaron – 'enlightened of God'; *Unwin* – 'non-friend'

The Natural

Have you ever watched a man
shag a black Labrador on a bed?
Or a woman on all fours take a donkey in the ass?
It doesn't seem that unnatural.

We kept a farm in UNDERWHELEM.
Those farm boys were mad
to shag anything, rubbed themselves
on sleepers, salt licks and the old hog oiler.

Aaron kept a goat's hoof in his pants
and pushed it down my vest.
I've seen many a grown man work his fist
up to the elbow in a sheep's muff.

The Natural

Have you ever watched a man
shag a black Labrador on a bed?
Or a woman on all fours take a donkey in the ass?
It doesn't seem that unnatural.

We kept a farm in UNDERWHELEM.
Those farm boys were mad
to shag anything, rubbed themselves
on sleepers, salt licks and the old hog oiler.

Aaron kept a goat's hoof in his pants
and pushed it down my vest.
I've seen many a grown man work his fist
up to the elbow in a sheep's muff.

sleeper – horizontal beams supporting and
spreading weight, for example, railway sleepers

Sheep

White purls of the Dorset Downs,
offspring of the mouflon womb.

Each with their individual cry
but silent when in pain.

Celestial mob. Sacrifices
with fleecy faces.

Sheep

White purls of the Dorset Downs,
offspring of the mouflon womb.

Each with their individual cry
but silent when in pain.

Celestial mob. Sacrifices
with fleecy faces.

purl – curl, swirl, frill, or an abbreviation of *pur lamb*;
mouflon – breed of sheep (the mouflon is thought to
be the ancestor for all modern domestic sheep breeds)

August
Gore Woods

The leaves fall
world wide.
All cross over
the other side.

Before I leave
someone please,
Love Me Tender
'neath the trees.

Lorn of leaf,
the twigs sigh.
Child and season
mortify.

August

Gore Woods

Tree-tears vall
wordle wide.
All'us cross o'er
t'other side.

'Vore I leave
someone please,
Love Me Tender
'neath the trees.

Lorn of leaf,
twiddicks sigh.
Child and season
mortify.

Twigs
Eight

Till the world's
will succumbs
Wander
in the idiom

Twiddicks

Aïght

Till the wordle's
will succumbs
Vokket
in the idiom

September

Ira asks: who is the saviour of beast and man? The misery of autumn term begins and Ira contemplates her twin nature. In Gore Woods Ira sees bad omens.

Twigs
Nine

Midges float on tiny sighs
Multiply I in their eyes
Hybrid hex-aroused rhymes
Stare I back a thousand times

Twiddicks

Nine

Air vlees vloat on tiny sighs
Multiply I in their eyes
Hybrid hex-arouséd rhymes
Stare I back a thousand times

A Place Through Which Everything Passes

In the woods she communes
with the ghosties of youth
through the arc of the oak
and scratches *I am.*

Baptised by the brook
and advised by the ash
and The Eye in the elm
unravels the world.

Who is the saviour of beast and of man?

Crowned by the hawthorn
circles the stations
and waits for the answer
by the red wallflowers.

Braced by the brambles
sways in the evening
becalling, mouthing,
Girl, daughter, woman.

Who is the saviour of beast and of man?

She takes a big sandwich,
peanut-butter, banana,
to Elvis-the-bleeder,
the ghostie-king Soldier.

A Place Through Which Everything Passes

In the woods she communes
with the sooneres of youth
through the arc of the woak
and scratches *I am*.

Baptised by the brook
and advised by the ash
and The Eye in the elm
unravels the world.

Who is the saviour of beast and of man?

Crowned by the hawthorn
circles the stations
and waits for the answer
by the bloody warriors.

Braced by the brembles
sways in the evemen
becalling, mouthing,
Girl, daughter, woman.

Who is the saviour of beast and of man?

She takes a big sandwich,
peanut-butter, banana,
to Elvis-the-bleeder,
the soonere-king Soldier.

Things I Found in Gore Woods: September 5th

White-throat, wren,
and a scatter-swarm
of starling-shards
upon the maker's magnet;
all of them leaving.

Things I Found in Gore Woods: September 5th

White-throat, cutty,
and a scatter-swarm
o' starling-shards
upon the maker's magnet;
all 'em leaving.

Autumn Term

At The Golden Fleece
I must ascend
three steps to hell.

The school bus
heaves back up the hill
and turns to OVERWHELEM.

Look behind yourself,
red eyed against
the window-mist.

Last week the ash
gifted their keys,
yet none will bring me freedom.

The woody nightshade
drooped her beads
and bade, Come feed on these.

The blackthorn spears
on Witches Mead
cussed, Come and lean on these!

At the school gates
I vomit Lamlac and sheep pellets
on Miss Goater's brogues.

Autumn Term

At The Golden Fleece
I must ascend
three steps to hell.

The school bus
heaves back up the hill
and turns to OVERWHELEM.

Look behind yourself,
red eyed 'gainst
the wilder-mist.

Last week the aish
gifted their keys,
yet none will bring me freedom.

The woody nightshade
drooped her beads
an' bade, Come feed on theosom.

The sloey spears
on Witches Mead
cussed, Come and lean on theosom!

At the dread gates
I vom Lamlac and sheep nuts
on Miss Goater's brogues.

Lamlac – lambs' formula milk powder

In Twain

Stacy Gale's unborn twin a-latched to her left ovary
and grew inside till Doctor Doyle made the strange discovery;

a weasel clot with half a face, a single tooth, and coséd eye,
and one long lock of blackest hair a-coiled around its scrawny thigh.

Once a ewe birthed on my head a sticky foetus all deformed,
as I was kneeling at her teat to milk her for her lamb firstborn.

Strange baptism of a sort, the claggy lump smeared o'er my head
as lonely hoof and woolly scraps; upon the straw it fell much dead.

Methinks my twin once grew inside, that tol'rable tup I could have been;
but, wether on the nether-edge, I quiver somewhere in between.

In Twain

Stacy Gale's unborn twin a-latchéd to her left egg-tree
and growed inside till Doctor Doyle made the strange discovery;

a veäre-sized clot with half a face, a single tooth, an' closéd eye,
and one long lock of blatchest hair a'rangled round its tewly thigh.

Once a ewe birthed on my head a clitty foetus all a'scram,
as I was kneeling at her tet to milk her for her firstborn lamb.

Strange baptism of a sort, the clodgy lump smoored o'er my poll
an' fell much dead upon the straw as lwonely hoof and scraps o' wool.

Methinks my twin once growed inside, that tarble tup I could have been;
but, wether on the nether-edge, I biver somewhere in-between.

Stacy – 'resurrection'; *Gale* – 'strange'; *Doyle* – 'strange'

Things I Found in Gore Woods: Michaelmas Day

A split oak gall:
A black spider,
A bad year,
Shortages,
A ruined harvest.

Things I Found in Gore Woods: Michaelmas Day

A split oak gall:
A black spider,
A bad year,
Shortages,
A ruined harvest.

If a 'worm' is found inside an oak gall on Michaelmas Day,
then the year will be pleasant and unexceptional; if a spider
is found, then it will be a bad year with shortages and ruined
crops; if a fly is found, then it will be a moderate season; if
nothing is found, then serious diseases will occur all that year

OCTOBER

The wealthy landowner Thomas Blaggot is buried on his horse in Gore Woods according to UNDERWHELEM folklore. Ira wants to know where. We track John Forsey — Ooser-Rod — and sniff the stinking iris. Randy the ram arrives to tup the ewes. We say a prayer for father Chalmers before going to the pub.

Things I Found in Gore Woods: October 1st

Seven magpies
conceal a secret:
brazen Blaggot,
upright on his stallion
ever-earthed in Gore.

Things I Found in Gore Woods: October 1st

Zebm chattermags
healin' a secret:
branten Blaggot,
upright on 'es rudger
ever-ethed in Gore.

devil's birds, chattermags – magpies; 'one for sorrow,
two for joy, three for a girl, four for a boy, five for
silver, six for gold, seven for a secret never to be told'

Devil

Gore Woods

Saplings search for palest sun
sickly rays through sullen elm
ground a grave for little souls:
dead leaves in the bunker holes
beige and ruby, green and fawn
oak and scarlet sycamore

Blaggot's Moon, toad-skin cold
ivy, moss and ferns enfold
still a few winged velvets fly:
sulphur, brimstone butterflies
hawk-moth casings, galls of oak
in the beech-grove, thrush and finch

Acorn feast for rooks and daws
dogs are barking, Forsey's saw
roars a warning, imps appear
a man-shaped mound, a feather tear
floats a hymn from heaven's dome:
Summer from his nest has flown

Wurse

Gore Woods

Saplings search for palest zun
tewly rays through sullen elm
ground a grave for little souls:
tree-tears in the bunker holes
beige and ruby, green and fawn
oak and scarlet sycamore

Blaggot's Moon, twoad-skin cold
ivy, meesh and ferns enfold
still a few winged velvets fly:
sulphur, brimstone vlutterbies
hawk-moth casings, galls of oak
in the beech grove, drush and mwope

Eacor feast for rooks and daws
dogs are barking, Forsey's saw
roars a warning, imps appear
a man-shaped mound, a feather tear
floats a hymn from heabm's dome:
Zummer from his nest has flown

Shotgun cartridge, bullock whip
sack of jute with arm-hole rips
a guise with head and horns complete
stinking elder dressed with meat,
rubber johnny, child-sized snare,
sticky locks of human hair

Shotgun cartridge, bullock whip
sack of jute with arm-hole rips
a guise with head and horns complete
stinking elder dressed with meat,
rubber johnny, child-sized snare,
clitty locks of human hair

elder dressed with meat – a remedy for warts: one should steal a bit
of raw beef and touch every wart with it, then hang it in the elder

Forsey Versey

axeman, wily nemesis
sprays his realm with mummer-jizz

hessian devil? horny god?
buffing up The Devil's-Cock

Forsey Vess'y

axeman, wily nemesis
sprays his realm with mummer-jizz

hessian wurse? horny god?
buffing up The Ooser-Rod

Sloven'y Versey

as I were stomping Gorey Lane
methinks I smelt some kippers

I asked the sloven what it was
she said it were her knickers

Slommocky Vess'y

as I were trapesèn Gorey Lane
methinks I smelt some kippers

I asked the slommock what it was
she said it were her knickers

Sloven-Mole Forsey

leans towards us over the wall
out from a lonesome fairy tale.
Her breath as fester-sweet as lure.

Pin-prick eyes, half-blind,
leak a little in the light;
a small tear for a dopey year

pushing a pram of sycamore,
and stumbling on her husband's fists.
Between her legs a never nest.

Her tangled tongue circles,
scraping out a shall-not-song
that grates long after she is gone;

Hasn't, hasn't. 'Tisn't, 'tisn't.
Cannot, cannot. Isn't, isn't.
Wasn't, wasn't. Mightn't, mightn't.

I mustn't.
I mustn't.

Slommock-Want Forsey

leans t'wards us over the wall
out from a lwonesome veäry tale.
Her breath as fester-sweet as lure.

Pin-prick eyes, half-blind,
leak a little in the light;
a small tear for a sa'tpoll year

pushing a pram of sycamore,
and stumbling on her husband's fists.
Between her legs a noowhen nest.

Her taffled tongue zircles,
scrooping out a shatten-song
that grates long after she is gone;

Hassen, hassen. Tidd'n, tidd'n.
Cas'n, cas'n. Bissen, bissen.
Ben't, ben't. Midn', midn'.

I mus'n.
I mus'n.

lure – a disease of sheep; an ulcer in the cleft of the foot

Twigs

Ten

Stinking iris, wild she grows
Take her inside with my nose
With my red tongue lick a leaf:
Perfumed curtains of roast beef

Twiddicks

Ten

Stinking iris, wild she grows
Inner take 'er with my nose
With my red rag lick a leaf:
Perfumed curtains of roast beef

curtains of roast beef – the scent of the stinking iris is likened to roast beef

Randy in Ecstasy

Thou shalt not turn thy back on the ram

He came rope-tied
to the back-seat
of Jack Chaffey's
Austin 55 Saloon

and spent the next
four years chasing
our fleeing arses
across the pasture.

He yearned to gore
anything that moved.
I think it gave him
Jim'll-fix-its.

Randy in Ecstasy

Thou shalt not turn thy back on the ram

He came rope-tied
to the back-seat
of Jack Chaffey's
Austin 55 Saloon

and spent the next
four years chasing
our fleeing arses
'cross the grotten.

He yearned to hook
anything that moved.
I think it gave him
Jim'll-fix-its.

Jim'll-fix-it — orgasm

Drunk as a Lord's Prayer

Ira's bastard versey

Our Farter, who art unshaven
Arseholed be thy Name
Thy Kingdom's done
Thy wool is spun
In Dorset as 'tis in Devon
Legless today and still in bed
All abrim with hooch sandwiches
As he's a pisshead that rages against us
And give me please up for adoption
As yer liver is pure evil
For vile is your Mingdom
Your glower and your fury
Shit-faced forever
Amen

Drunk as a Lord's Prayer

Ira's bastard vess'y

Our Farter, who art unshaven
Arseholed be thy Name
Thy Kingdom's done
Thy wool is spun
In Darzet as 'tis in Devon
Legless today and still in bed
All abrim with hooch sandwiches
As e's a pisshead that tilties against us
And give me please up for adoption
As yer liver is sclerevil
For vile is yer Mingdom
Yer glower and yer fury
Shit-faced forever
Amen

The Golden Fleece

Underneath a Blaggot's Moon
its empty frame swings in the wind
at the crossing of two hollow roads

while the babysat of UNDERWHELEM

Across the small bar Chalmers drinks
with Doug Leathermewell, Doctor Doyle
The Knackers Man and Rick the Brick

while the babysat of UNDERWHELEM
pray the dread door does not open

The pig-faced landlord drawls *Here 'tis*,
to Jack Chaffey and Paul the Horse
and stinks of Palmers and billy goat jizz

while the babysat of UNDERWHELEM
pray the dread door does not open
on Dogwell's creaky landing

The Golden Fleece

Underneath a Blaggot's Moon
its empty frame swings in the wind
at the crossing of two gawly roads

while the over-watched of UNDERWHELEM

Athirt the small bar Chalmers drinks
with Doug Leathermewell, Doctor Doyle
The Knackers Man and Rick the Brick

while the over-watched of UNDERWHELEM
pray the dread door does not open

The pig-faced landlord dreans *Yer tiz*,
to Jack Chaffey and Paul the Horse
and stinks of Palmers and billy goat jizz

while the over-watched of UNDERWHELEM
pray the dread door does not open
on Dogwell's creaky landing

NOVEMBER

At the sunset of the year we walk with Ira in Gore Woods at midnight on All Souls. Wyman-Elvis has disappeared. On Bonfire Night Ira burns a twig doll of her father.

Twigs

Eleven

Hail the sunset of the year,
Crimson on The Soldier's tears.
Tender silence veil our Gore;
Shroud I o'er in never-more.

Twiddicks

Elebm

Hail the sunset of the year,
Crimson on The Soldier's tears.
Neshen silence heal our Gore;
Shroud I o'er in never-more.

All Souls

Gore Woods

A carnival, a flesh farewell.
Omens rising from the dead.
Wyman-Elvis! calls our girl,
And counts the ash to where he bled:

At the first a crimson mist,
At the second sleeplessness.
At the third a broken tryst,
At the fourth, lonesomeness.

Hollow in the goose-grass leaves.
Hollow in the soldier's tears.
As the Riddle river grieves:
Wyman-Elvis disappears . . .

Only in a scrap of flesh
Hooked upon the hart's-tongue fern,
And only by her own gooseflesh
Knows she sometime he'll return.

All Souls
Gore Woods

A carnival, a flesh farewell.
Heissens rising from the dead.
Wyman-Elvis! calls our gurrel,
And counts the ash to where he bled:

At the first a crimson mist,
At the second sleeplessness.
At the third a broken tryst,
At the fourth, lwonesomeness.

Gawly in the sweethearts leaves.
Gawly in the soldier's tears.
As the Riddle river grieves:
Wyman-Elvis disappears . . .

Only in a scrid of flesh
Hooked upon the hart's-tongue fern,
And only by her own gooseflesh
Knows she somewhen he'll return.

Bonfire Night

'Neath the fir trees hidden
I stare into the kitchen
and see the thing I'm after
hauling 'cross the chamber
his shadow like a lea,
or a sack of sheep.

Frightened on the doorstep,
I enter very quiet,
as daddy-bad-meat looms
beside the roasting tomb,
and shoves a rump of boy-lamb
into the bottom oven.

Clutchéd to my little ribs
is his effigy in twigs:
a home-made father-Fawkes
to burn black in the clearing,
and later, hid by dusk
uncover I the doll

and poke into its centre
some mutton for his liver
and a curl between his teeth
so when he's naught but dust
I am released forever
onto the edge of nether.

Bonfire Night

Hidden 'neath the vuzzen
I glow into the kitchen
and see the thing I'm after
hauling 'cross the chammer
'es shadow like a leaze,
or a zack o' theaves.

Flummocksed on the doorstep,
I enter brushen quiet,
as daddy-cag-mag looms
beside the roasting tomb,
and shoves a rump o' pur lamb
into the bottom oven.

Clutchéd to my riblets is
a mommet-dad of twiddicks:
a-sembled father-Fawkes
to charken in the gawl,
and later, hid by dummet
unheal I the mommet

an poke into its centre
some mutton for 'es liver
an' a curdle 'tween 'es teeth
so when 'e's nowt but smeech
I am released forever
onto the edge of nether.

Things I Found in Gore Woods: November 5th

A doll of sticks
a dangling Dad
hanging from the alder's crook.
The white ash fire
Loves Me Tender.

Things I Found in Gore Woods: November 5th

A pwope of scroff
a dangling Dad
hanging from the aller's scrag.
The white aish fire
Loves Me Tender.

Chalmers-Adam Rawles

I watched him shrink
to pelt and bone,
poisoned by diazinon,
crippled by a crooked nail,
charred black by a doll of sticks;
on a rank bed of pigeon feathers
with blowflies all at feast
he cried like a sick lamb
that no teat can nurse,
but I didn't sob,
and shamelessly, I prayed:
Thy Kingdom's done.
Thy wool is spun.

Chalmers-Adam Rawles

I watched en shrink
to pelt and bwone,
poisoned by diazinon,
crippled by a crooked nail,
charked by a scroff doll;
on a rank bed of culver feathers
with vlesh vlees all a'teare
'e bleared like a lamb wi' lear
that no tet can nursy,
but I didden sify,
and un-chawly-whist, I prayed:
Thy Kingdom's done.
Thy wool is spun.

Chalmers – lord of the household; *Adam* – man, to be
red, earth; *Rawle(s)* – 'rad', counsel, advice, and 'wolf'

Things I Found in Gore Woods: November 26th

Mole-hands digging
upwards from my innards
to my little mouth.
Out comes a cry:
Father!

Things I Found in Gore Woods: November 26th

Want-hands huming
upwards from my inwards
to my little gap.
Out comes a cry:
Father!

I Inside the Old Year Dying
Gore Woods

Sun's a feeble lamp
O'er famished land

Starlings chat in code
Lark a meagre note

Thrush repeats himself
Over UNDERWHELEM

Hunkered in the ruins
Shepherd girl grief-sways:

I in the lost lane calling Mary
I in the silence of the hole
I inside the old year dying
I in each leaf as it falls

I in the lost lane calling Mary
I in the silence of the earth
I inside the old year dying
On I march to my child-death

I Inside the Old Year Dying

Gore Woods

Zun's a feeble lamp
O'er leery land

Stares a'chat in code
Lark a meagre note

Drush repeats 'enself
Over UNDERWHELEM

Croopied in the reames
Shepherd gurrel weaves:

I in the holway calling Mary
I in the silence of the gawl
I inside the old year dying
I in each leaf as it valls

I in the holway calling Mary
I in the silence of the eth
I inside the old year dying
Vore-right I to my chile-death

December

At the year's end Ira remembers her lamb, Mallory-Sonny, and searches again for her mother, Lola. The sheep now instruct Ira with The Word. As she enters adulthood her child joins the dead soonere-children, the Ash-Wraiths, and patiently awaits Wyman's return.

Things I Found in Gore Woods: December 1st

A mocking thrush in the tangled yew.
A seance o' sheep beneath the oak.
A lone blackbird,
a hooded crow.
The masked man in a jute-sack cloak.

Things I Found in Gore Woods: December 1st

A dorring drush in the caddled yew.
A seance o' theaves beneath the woak.
A darkling bird,
a hooded crow.
The masked man in a jute-sack cloak.

Mallory-Sonny

Nine tears when I found him
like a pile of rags
by a pen of thorns.

Cast out by his mother
I fed him Lamlac
from a plastic teat,

but alone in the field
the black bards got him.
Whenever I thereafter

cowered before a fist
I saw his blue tongue
and gone eyeball

the leg torn from the hip
as I blooded my hands
in his gut-strings

and raised them to my lips.

Mallory-Sonny

Nine tears when I found him
like a pile of rags
by a pleck of thorns.

Cast out by his mother
I fed him Lamlac
from a plastic tet,

but loneleft in the grotten
the black bards got him.
Whenever I thereafter

croopied 'vore a fist
I saw his blue tongue
and gone eyeball

the lag torn from the hip
as I blooded my hands
in his gut-strings

and raised them to my lips.

black bards – rooks, also known as 'storytellers'

Lola-Effie Colby
Gore Woods

I see her in the north-east corner,
Lola of sorrows, beautifully silent.

My sadness seeks her out.
I carve into the oak,

Mother Forever
Together Alone

Lola-Effie Colby

Gore Woods

I see her in the north-east corner,
Lola of sorrows, beautifully silent.

My sadness seeks her out.
I scratch into the oak,

Mother Forever
Together Alone

Lola – 'sorrows'; *Effie* – 'beautiful silence';
Colby – 'from the dark farmstead'

The Woolly Messengers of The Word

The wethers are my favourites –
poor, fattened hoggets
unsexed and sent early to Loveless's yard.

I kneel to eat their coarse-mix pellets,
string hag-stones for them in their stalls,
feel them for comfort, for The Word.

On Christmas Eve
blessed with their annual gift of speech
they fell to their knees

and turned to the east of the forest:
Love Him Tender
Love Him Tender

The Woolly Messengers of The Word

The wethers are my favourites –
poor, fattened hoggets
unsexed and sent early to Loveless's yard.

I kneel to eat their coarse-mix pellets,
string hag-stones for them in their stalls,
feel them for comfort, for The Word.

On Christmas Eve
blessed with their annual gift of speech
they fell to their knees

and turned to the east of the forest:
Love Him Tender
Love Him Tender

coarse-mix pellets – sheep food; *hag-stone* – a stone with a natural
hole through it. These are often believed to ward off the dead,
curses, witches, sickness, and nightmares; *On Christmas Eve* –
tradition has it that at this time cattle turn to the east and kneel to
adore the child in the manger; during the Christmas season cattle
received the gift of speech, but it is dangerous to listen to them

Twigs
Twelve

Ira never feels more right
Gadding in the Gorey night
If I die before I'm home
Sink I in the forest loam

Twiddicks

Twelve

Ira never feel more right
Vokket in the Gorey night
If I die before I'm hwome
Grave I in the forest loam

I Inside the Old I Dying

Gore Woods

Oak and beech buds wait.
The velvet ash buds wait.
Frogs and toads in logwood holes
and hedgehogs in their leafy ditch,
all waiting for His kingdom.

Wyman, Wyman,
Love Me Tender . . .

Earth waits.
The dead brakes
host the holly-berries;
they are His crown of thorns
and He will rise again.

Wyman, Wyman . . .
Undress I for him,
slip from my childhood skin;
I sing through the forest,
I hover in the hollow lane,

I laugh in the leaves
and merge into moss,
just a song in the oak
with the chalky children
of evermore.

I Inside the Old I Dying

Gore Woods

Woak and beech buds wait.
The velvet aish buds wait.
Frogs and twoads in lagwood holes
and hedgehogs in their leafy ditch,
all waiting for His kingdom.

Wyman, Wyman,
Love Me Neshen . . .

Eth waits.
The dead brakes
host the holm's blood beads;
they are His crown of thorns
and He will rise again.

Wyman, Wyman . . .
Unray I for en,
slip from my childhood skin;
I zing through the forest,
I hover in the holway,

I laugh in the leaves
and merge into meesh,
just a charm in the woak
with the chalky children
of evermore.

Things I Found in Gore Woods: December 31st

Lola wandering in her sleep.
Cade lambs bleating from the steep.
A thousand children dressed in white,
a ghost-song from the other side;
Tender Love, till Never's Tide.

Things I Found in Gore Woods: December 31st

Lola wandering in her sleep.
Orphans blethering from the steep.
A thousand children dressed in white,
a chalky charm from t'other side;
Tender Love, till Never's Tide.

January

With the new-born year Ira is reunited with Wyman-Elvis her Christ, her tender love, and bearer of The Word.

Prayer at the Gate

January 1st, Gore Woods

As childhood died the new-born year
made The Soldier reappear.

The ash embowered night and day
as at the five-bar gate she prayed;

Wyman-Elvis, am I worthy?
Wyman, speak your world to me.

Elms unveiled in secret places
a thousand ghostie-children's faces

and mist enshrouded in its cloak
lost lane, river, brook and oak,

and all souls under Orlam's reign
made passage for the *born again*.

So look before and look behind
at life and death all intertwined

and reach towards your dark-haired Lord
forever bleeding with The Word.

Prayer at the Gate

January 1st, Gore Woods

As childhood died the new-born year
made The Soldier reappear.

The ash embowered night and day
as at the five-bar gate she prayed;

Wyman-Elvis, am I worthy?
Wyman, speak your wordle to me.

Elms unveiled in secret places
a thousand soonere-children's faces

and drisk enshrouded in its cloak
holway, river, brook and oak,

and all souls under Orlam's reign
made passage for the *born again*.

So look before and look behind
at life and death all innertwined

and teake towards your dark-haired Lord
forever bleeding with The Word.

Glossary

a-cothed	rotten or diseased in the liver
aïght	eight
air vlees	flies that seldom land for hovering in the air
aish, aishy	ash tree
aish-a-twiddick	ash twig
aller	alder
allum	all of them
archet	orchard
a-sembled	made in the semblance of
a-stooded	sunk into the ground, as a cartwheel or fencepost
athirt	across, over
auverlook	overlook, bewitch, look on with the evil eye
avore, 'vore	before
a-zew	dry of milk, no longer giving suck
b'aint	be not
bandon, bandoned	abandonment, abandoned
bandy	crooked, bent
bantling	child
bedraggled angels	wet sheep
ben't	wasn't
biddle	beetle
bissen	bist not, art not
biver	to shake or quiver with cold or fear
black bards	rooks, also known as 'storytellers'
black-bob	cockroach
blatch	black
bleare	to cry loud and fretful like a child

blether	to bleat or blare much; to talk noisily
blood beads	berries
bloody warriors	wallflowers
braims	membranes
brake	a thicket
branten	bold, impudent
brembles	brambles
brickley	brittle
brushen	huge, giant
bull-head	tadpole
bundle	to bound quickly
bunker	rabbit
butt	a clashing, bumping or hitting together
button-crawler	woodlouse
bwone	bone
bwoneyard	graveyard, churchyard
caddle	entanglement, muddle
cag	cloy, clog
cag-mag	rotten meat
cammish	awkward
carner	corner
cas'n	can'st not
cast	prematurely born
chalky	ghostly
chammer	chamber, bedroom, room
charken, charked	burn (to charcoal), burned
charm	a noise or confusion of voices, as in children or birds; a spell
chattermag	magpie
chawly-whist	ashamed
chetlens	the entrails of any edible animal

chilver, chilver hog	a yearling ewe lamb
clitty	stringy and sticky, tangled in clods or lumps
clodgy	dumplike, close
clot	lump, clod
clutchéd	clutched
codgloves	hedger's gloves, with a bag for all the fingers together
comely, come	to be ripe, inviting
conk-load	nose-full
conzum-ed	consumed
cowheart	coward
crate	womb
creezey	silky
crewel	cowslip
crims	cold-shivers, creeping of flesh
croodle	to rock, to coo, to make little crowings
croopy	to sink one's body, bending down the thighs behind the legs
culver	wood pigeon
curdle, curdled	curl, curled
cutty	wren
dank	damp
dark	blind, dark
darkling bird	blackbird
daw	jackdaw
death-biddle	deathwatch beetle
de-da	simple, foolish, slow-witted
devil's bird	magpie
didden	did not
dorring	mocking
draty	draught, draughty, full of draughts of air

dread-fulled	full of dread
dread gates	school gates
drean	to drawl in speaking
dree	three
drisk	a fine, wind-driven mist
drownsy	drowned
drush	thrush
dumble, dumbledore	bumblebee
dummet	dusk
dungy	downcast, dull
dunnick	sparrow
'e	he
eacor	acorn
egg-tree	ovary
elebm	eleven
eltroot	cow parsley
em	them
en	him
engripement	grievance
'enself	himself
'es	his
'e's	he is
eth, ethly	earth, earthly
ethed	buried
ether-hunger	the hunger for earth, sometimes felt by persons approaching death
evemen	evening
fallow	fallow deer
farterous	father-like
feasen	faces

femboy	a girly guy
Feverell	February
fleeceful	as much as fills a fleece
fleecy	fleece; drunk, drunken
flummocks	to overcome, frighten, bewilder
fowel	the placenta of a cow
freen	free from
frog-hopper	grasshopper
furby	foul or sticky matter, as that on a tongue in sickness
gap	mouth
gapmouth	nightjar
gawl, gawly	an opening, an empty place, a bare patch; empty, hollow
geate	gate
ghost moth	*Hepialus humuli*
gi'e	to give, to yield
giltcup	buttercup
girding	taunting
glory hole	vagina
glow	stare or watch with fixed, open eyes
gnang	to mock by half-clear sounds, wagging the jaw with a grin
god's stinking tree	elder
goocoo	cuckoo
goocoo pint	cuckoo-pint, wild arum, snakeshead, *Arum maculatum*
goocoo's bread	wood sorrel
goocoo spettle, spume	cuckoo spit, a white froth secreted by insects
Gore	Gore Woods
grab	crab apple tree

gramf'er	grandfather
gramm'er	grandmother
grave	to bury; a grave
greaze	grease
greygle	bluebell
gribble	a young crab tree or blackthorn
grotten	a sheep-slade, a run or pasture for sheep
growed	grew
gurrel	girl
hag-ridden	a nightmare attributed to a supernatural presence of a witch or hag, by whom one is ridden in sleep
hangen house	a shed under the continuation of the roof of the house
hard-worken	industrious
harled	tangled
hassen	hast not
heabm	heaven
heal, healéd	to cover over; to hide; to bury
heissen	a prediction of evil
hetful	hot
heth	hearth
hidy-buck	the game of hide and seek
hoar-stone	standing stone or ancient boundary stone
hobble	a field-shed for cattle
hogget	a yearling sheep of either sex, the meat of a hogget
hogget shears	sheep shears
hold wi'	side with
hollow	valley
holm	holly

holrod	cowslip
holway	hollow lane
honking	inhale deeply
hook	to gore with the horns
ho's adder	dragonfly
huff	bully
huming	exhuming
hummock	cow
hustle	to moan, spoken of the wind
hwome	home
inneath	behind, inside
innertwined	intertwined
inwards	innards
knog	knob
lag	leg
lagwood	the larger cut-off branches and twigs of a tree
laminger	one who has become lame
lear	an ailing in sheep
leaze	field
leery	empty in the stomach, wanting food
let	a stopping or interruption
litty	of light and easy bodily motion
loneleft	left alone
long tail	pheasant
lovesome	lovely, loving
lowsen	to listen
lure	a disease of sheep; an ulcer in the cleft of the foot
lwone, lwonely	lone, lonely
lwonesomness	lonesomeness

maggoty	very drunk
mampus	a great number
mandy	saucy
mare's tail	*Equisetum arvense*, also known as horsetail
mazzerdy	knotty
meeces	mice
meesh	moss
midn'	might not, may not
milchi	milk, milky, pale
milk flower	snowdrop
mingdom	a stinking, dirty or unpleasant kingdom
mommet	a guy, an effigy
moule	field mouse
muff	vagina
munter, minger	extremely ugly person
mus'n	must not
mutton chops	sideburns
mwope	bullfinch
nammet	a luncheon (*Anglo-Saxon non-mete*, noon meat)
nearen	nearby
nesh, neshen	tender
nesseltripe	the weakest or last born
nether-ethed	buried
netherwise	viewed from below
no-but	nothing but
noowhen	at no time
not	hornless, as a not cow, not sheep
nursy	nurse, nursing, nursery
nuts	joy; testicles
onlook	to watch

oone	one
orf	a viral form of pustular dermatitis found in sheep, and communicable to humans
over-watch	baby-sit
owl, owling	to owl about, to ramble by night
Palmers	Dorset beer
pank	to pant
parlour-sky	attic, loft
peart	lively, quick, pert, saucy, in good health and spirits
pecker	green woodpecker
pelt	rage, fit of anger
peze, peaze	to ooze out
piss-a-bed	dandelion
pleck	a small enclosure
'plexion	complexion
pock-fretten	pock-marked from acne
poll	head
purl	curl, swirl, frill; or an abbreviation of *pur lamb*
pur lamb	a castrated ram lamb
puxy	a miry or boggy place
pwope	a bunchy thing, an effigy, a doll, a puppet
quartere'il, quaterevil	a disease of sheep, a corruption of the blood
rafty	rancid
rake	to reek
rammish	strong smelling, rank
rangle	to reach about like a trailing or climbing plant
reames	the frame or ligaments of a thing, skeleton
reapy	reap
red-bread	vagina

reddick	robin
red rag	tongue
reeve	to unravel
riblets	little ribs
ringworm	a fungus on the skin caught from livestock
roasting tomb	stove
rod	penis
ruddle	a red earth by which they mark sheep
rudger, or rig	uncastrated horse
rum	queer
rumstick	queer, a queer man
sar	to serve or feed animals
sarch	to search
sa'tpoll	soft poll, soft in the head
sclerevil	hardened and evil
scote	to shoot along very fast
scrag	a very crooked branch of a tree
scram	screwy-grown
scratch, scratching	to write, writing; to carve
screak, screaking	to creak loudly
scriddick, scrid	a small scrap or shred
scrip	shepherd's coat
scroff	small bits of dead wood
scroop, scrooping	the low sound of one hard body scraping against another
scrounch, scrunch	to crunch strongly
seem an I	seems to me
shabby mothers	ewes
shade	spirit, ghost
shatten	shall not
sheep nuts	coarse mix pellets, sheep food

shim	a she/him
shockle	to shake about lightly
shoo	a cry to fray away owls
shram	a screwing up or out of the body and limbs from keen cold
sify	to catch the breath in sighing; to sob
skeat, skeating	a looseness of the bowels
sloey spears	the sharp spines on the branches of the sloe or blackthorn
slommock(en)	a slatternly, thick-set, stocky, short, dirty woman
smame	to smear
smeech	a smoke-like body of dust
smirchéd	tarnished
smoor	to smear
snake's-head	*Arum maculatum*
so't	soft
soldier's tears	mullein, a tall, stiff flowered, woolly plant
somen	someone
somewhen	at some time
soonere	ghost
spawl, spawly	a splinter flown off, as from wood or stone; splintered
speare	thin, lanky
spet	to spit
spiles	the beard of barley
spotter	spotted woodpecker
spume	come, semen
squitters	diarrhoea in cattle
stare	starling
stiver	to stiffen up much as an angry dog's hairs
stumble fuck	a drunk
stumpy	to walk with short stamping steps

sweethearts	goose grass
sweven	a dream
taffle	to tangle, as grass or corn beaten down by weather
tarble	tolerable
tardle	to tangle
teake to	to reach forth to a man or thing with a ready good will
teare	eager and bold as flies on food
tet	teat
tewly	small and weakly
theave	a three-year-old sheep
theosom	these
thick as inkle weavers	close as in friendship, from *inkle*, a kind of tape for a very narrow loom at which the weavers sat close side by side
thieves	fairies
thik	that
thirtover	perverse
thumbles	thumbs
tidd'n	'tis not
tilty	a fit of anger
'tis	it is
t'other	the other
trapes, trapesèn	a woman who tramps about boldly
tree-tears	leaves
tuen	tune
tup	a ram; (of a ram) to copulate with a ewe
twanketen	melancholy
t'wards	towards
'twere	it were

twiddick	a small twig
twink	chaffinch
twoad	toad
twoad's meat	toadstools
undercreepen	underhand, working slyly against another
unheal	to uncover
unray	to undress
upsmitten	dust or liquid sprayed or blown upwards
vall	to fall
veag	wrath, a high heat of anger *(Anglo-Saxon faegth)*
veäre	weasel
veäry	fairy
veäry ring	fairy ring, a ring of fungi
veäry tale	fairy tale
vess'y	to versey, to read verses by turns
vilthy	filthy
vive	five
vlee	fly
vlesh vlee	a blowfly, a flesh fly
vlit	flit
vlittermouse	bat
vloat	float
vlutterbie	butterfly
vog	fog
vokket	to go about here and there
voley	vole
vom	vomit
vorehearing	premonition, forewarning
vore-right	going forward without regard to consequences or seemliness

voretold	foretold
vorewarn	forewarned
voul	foul, loathsome
vower, vowr, vow'r	four
vuzzen	fir trees
wagwanton	quaking grass
want	mole
want-heave	mole hill
want-heave slave	a mole
waxen crundels	swollen tonsils
weave	to rock backwards and forwards as in pain
wether	a castrated male lamb
wevvet	cobweb
wevvet queens	spiders
wheel-bird	nightjar
whinnick	to whine softly or slightly
whiver	to hover, to quiver
wilder mist	steam on a widow
winker	eyeball
woak	oak
woodculver	the wood pigeon or ringdove
woone	one
wops	wasp
wordle	world
wordle-wide	worldwide
wurse	devil, arch-fiend, a variation of 'Ooser'
yer	your
yer tiz	here it is, yes it is
yis	worm
yoller	yellow

yollerheads	daffodils
yoller roses	primroses
zack	sack
zebm	seven
zedgemocks	tufts of sedge grass
zing	sing
zive	sycthe
zix	six
zixty	sixty
zounds	sounds
zummer	summer
zun	sun
zwail	to swagger, to sway about from side to side
zweal	to scorch
zweat	sweat
zweem, zweemy	a feeling of swinging around in the head

Acknowledgements

My greatest thanks to my editor, mentor, and friend Don Paterson who helped me bring this book into existence, and to my mother Eva Jean Harvey for her close reading, support, guidance and love, without which none of this could have happened.

Thank you to my managers at ATC, Brian Message and Sumit Bothra, for their belief in me and the work, and for enabling its creation.

Thank you to Stuart Wilson for his masterly design, and to Michelle Henning and Sumit Bothra for their assistance in the design process.

Thanks to Ann Harrison; thanks to my dear friends Leigh Message, John Parish, Ruth Wilson, Sophocles Maraveyas, Ann Demeulemeester and Patrick Robyn. Thanks to Jon Glazer, Ian Rickson, Ben Whishaw, Colin Morgan and Todd Lynn for their readings of the work as it developed, and their feedback which helped me enormously.

I am indebted to the great William Barnes for his *Glossary of the Dorset Dialect*.

Credits

Picador

Publisher Philip Gwyn Jones
Editor Don Paterson
Communications Alice Dewing
Editorial Assistant Salma Begum
Copyediting and proofreading Nicholas Blake
Contracts Marta Dziurosz
Sales Rory O'Brien, Richard Green, Emily Scorer

PJ Harvey

Management Brian Message & Sumit Bothra, ATC Management
Management Team Olivia Plunket, Aimy Marling and Harprit Johal
Legals Ann Harrison
Accounts David Lewis & Julie Hodge, RSM

Design and Production

Illustrations PJ Harvey
Cover Design and Product Designer Stuart Wilson
Design Consultants Michelle Henning & Sumit Bothra
Illustration Photography Peter Mallet
Head of Production Simon Rhodes
Senior Production Controller Giacomo Russo
Text Design Manager Lindsay Nash
Typesetter Rachel Smyth